HISTORY NOTES

S. Ross Doughty

Ursinus College

THE WORLD'S HISTORY, VOLUME I:

PREHISTORY TO 1500

THIRD EDITION

Howard Spodek

Temple University

PEARSON

Prentice
Hall

Upper Saddle River, New Jersey 07458

© 2006 by PEARSON EDUCATION, INC.
Upper Saddle River, New Jersey 07458

ISBN 0-13-177347-X

Printed in the United States of America

Contents

1   THE DRY BONES SPEAK
5 million B.C.E. – 10,000 B.C.E.

KEY TOPICS
- **Human Origins in Myth and History**
- **Fossils and Fossil Hunters**
- **Humans Create Culture**

CHAPTER NOTES

In the space provided below, construct your own outline of the chapter. Before you begin, refer to the "Key Topics" (section headings – above), introductory paragraph, chapter conclusion ("The Story of Prehistory: What Difference Does It Make"?) and "Review Questions" to help you identify the major questions and issues covered in the chapter and the author's main arguments and interpretations. This will aid you in deciding what to include in your outline notes.

TRUE/FALSE QUESTIONS: Read each question carefully (answers at end of chapter).

1. The hominid species *Homo habilis,* who lived approximately 1.8 million years ago, was given its name because of their ability to construct habitations or shelters for themselves. ___
2. The migration of human beings throughout the world was facilitated by the existence of land bridges that extended and connected major land masses during the last Ice Age. ___
3. The term "myth" refers to an interpretive story of the past that cannot be verified historically but has a deep moral message. ___
4. Modern anthropologists disagree on the question of the geographical origins of *Homo erectus*: while some believe the species first evolved in Africa, others believe the process began elsewhere. ___
5. "Venus Figurines," small prehistoric statuettes of female bodies, are thought to be representations of ideal feminine beauty. ___
6. "Lucy" was the name given to one of the earliest Venus Figurines discovered in Africa. ___
7. Because the total amount of radiocarbon (Carbon 14) in any organism is small, little of it remains after 40,000 years and the method is useless for dating any objects more than 70,000 years old. ___
8. The term "exogamous marriage" refers to a form of incest that was practiced by isolated early hunter-gatherer bands. ___
9. Anthropologists now believe that Neanderthal hominids were closely related to *Homo sapiens sapiens* and looked very much like us. ___
10. "Shamans" – persons thought to be able to communicate with spirits through trances induced by drugs, breathing exercises, and rhythmic singing, dancing or clapping – have existed in many prehistoric societies in Asia, Africa and the Americas. ___

MULTIPLE CHOICE: Select the response that completes the sentence or answers the question best:

1. According to paleoanthropologists, which of the following was <u>not</u> a characteristic of "women's work" in prehistoric times?
    a. Women's work was easily interruptible and easily resumed.
    b. Women's work was not dangerous to their children.
    c. Women's work required less skill than men's work.
    d. Women's work did not require the participant's total concentration.

2. Charles Darwin and Alfred Russell Wallace argued that different species had evolved:
    a. Through the separate creation of individual species.
    b. As animals produced new organs to adapt to changing environmental needs.
    c. Through metamorphosis from lower forms of life.
    d. Through a process of "natural selection" or "survival of the fittest."

3. Virtually all paleoanthropologists now agree that our hominid ancestor *Homo erectus* evolved first in:
    a. Java
    b. Africa
    c. China
    d. Germany

4. The research of Charles Darwin is a textbook example of which of the following?
    a. Paleoanthropology
    b. "Normal science"
    c. "Scientific revolution"
    d. Teleology

5. The revision of early 20th century conceptions of Neanderthals represents an example of which process?
    a. Teleology
    b. "Scientific revolution"
    c. "Political correctness"
    d. "Normal science"

6. Which of the following characteristics is typical of <u>all</u> hominid species?
    a. Bipedalism, or the ability to walk upright
    b. The tendency to live in river valleys
    c. Facility in tool-making
    d. The continuing development of brain capacity after birth

7. Paleoanthropologists have calculated the optimum size of stone-age hunter-gatherer bands at approximately 25 people each, based largely on the study of:
    a. Surviving hunter-gatherers
    b. Carbon 14
    c. Mitochondrial DNA
    d. Fossil skeletons

8. Creation myths such as those found in the *Enuma Elish* of Mesopotamia, India's *Rigveda* and the Hebrew *Bible*:
    a. Have a teleological purpose
    b. Are unprovable, because they begin at a time before humans existed
    c. Provide people with an explanation of the meaning of their existence
    d. All of the above

9. To date, the earliest known hominid remains that have been discovered have been classified as:
    a. *Homo neanderthalensis*
    b. *Homo erectus*
    c. *Australopithecus afarensis*
    d. *Ardipithecus ramidus*

10. Which of the following discoveries was <u>not</u> among the achievements of the Leakey family?
    a. The initial discovery of *Australopithecus afarensis*, a.k.a. "Lucy"
    b. The footprints at Laetoli, confirming that *Australopithecus afarensis* walked upright
    c. The discovery of *Homo habilis*, a.k.a. "handy person"
    d. *Zinjanthropus boisei*, an early ape fossil

11. "Ice Ages" – periods of severe global cooling – are believed to have begun particularly important eras of:
    a. Human migration
    b. Language development
    c. Early artistic creativity
    d. Agricultural development

12. The "Candelabra Theory" of human evolution argues that the evolution of *Homo sapiens*:
    a. Occurred through the inheritance of newly developed organs
    b. Occurred only in Africa
    c. Occurred in many different regions
    d. Occurred through the process of thermoluminescense

13. The term "culture" is used to refer to the way *Homo sapiens* and their relatives:
    a. Used art to depict their religious deities
    b. Evolved through natural selection
    c. Adapted to and shaped their environment
    d. Developed larger brain capacities

14. Noam Chomsky argued that the human capacity for language:
    a. Is biologically determined in the brain
    b. Has been developed through cultural evolution
    c. Is necessary for the acceleration of human development
    d. All of the above

15. The archaeological terms Paleolithic, Mesolithic and Neolithic refer specifically to:
    a. Stages in human biological evolution
    b. Stages in the development of language
    c. Stages in the development of tools made of stone
    d. Stages in the increasing sophistication of cave art

MAP ANALYSIS: The following exercise is based on the maps in Spodek, pp. 8, 23, and 24. Use the outline map below to complete the questions.

1. Using the map ("Human ancestors") on p. 8 of the text, mark and label the areas with the heaviest concentration of early hominid fossil discoveries on the outline map (opposite). Locate and identify the following places:
    a. Areas where the Leakey family made important discoveries
    b. The place where archaeologist Donald Johanson discovered *Australopithecus afarensis*
    c. The sites where remains of *Homo erectus* and Neaderthal hominids have been unearthed

2. Using the same map ("Human ancestors") – and the charts on pp. 16 and 18 of the text – draw and label alternative migration patterns illustrating the two opposing theories of hominid expansion and distribution (the "Candelabra" and "Noah's Ark" theories) on the outline map. How do they differ from one another?

3. Using the maps on p. 23 ("Early Humans in the Ice Age") and p. 24 ("The colonization of the Pacific"), mark and label the areas that were settled by *Homo sapiens* as a result of the last "Ice Age".

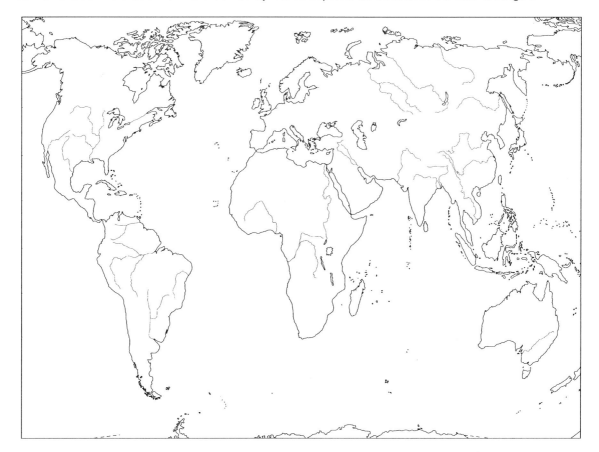

STUDY QUESTIONS: Consider each of the following questions carefully. Be prepared to supply specific evidence and examples to support your points in a class discussion or concise, well-organized written essay.

1. List and explain the three competing interpretations of how *Homo sapiens sapiens* was able to survive and eventually displace other hominids.

2. In the evolutionary process of natural selection, who or what does the selecting? In other words, how are the "fittest" determined for "survival of the fittest"? What are the implications of Darwin's theory, as opposed to those of the creation myths, regarding humans' relationship with their natural environment, other animals and each other?

3. According to the text, the difference between myth and history is that myths are "not supported by known facts." How do paleoanthropologists "know" what they know about human evolution? What different kinds of evidence and tools of research have been used by them to piece together the history of hominid biological and cultural development?

HOW DO WE KNOW?

The following questions are based on the various illustrations or quotations and extracts from primary source documents and historical interpretations in the chapter.

1. Using specific examples from illustrations in the text, discuss the various interpretations and explanations of the possible functions and purposes of art in prehistoric cultures.

2. According to anthropologist Sally Slocum, on what basis were gender roles determined in hunter-gatherer societies? What may have been some of the consequences of this role determination for the study of anthropology and history?

3. Using examples from the *Enuma Elish,* the *Rigveda*, and the *Bible*, explain the functions of creation myths in early societies. Cite specific passages or elements of the respective myths to illustrate your points.

TRUE/FALSE ANSWERS: 1-F; 2-T; 3-T; 4-F; 5-F; 6-F; 7-T; 8-F; 9-T; 10-T

MULTIPLE CHOICE ANSWERS: 1-C; 2-D; 3-B; 4-C; 5-D; 6-A; 7-A; 8-D; 9-A; 10-D; 11-A; 12-C; 13-C; 14-A; 15-C

2   FROM VILLAGE COMMUNITY TO CITY-STATE
10,000 B.C.E – 750 B.C.E.

KEY TOPICS
- **The Agricultural Village**
- **The First Cities**
- **Sumer: The Birth of the City**
- **The Growth of the City-State**

CHAPTER NOTES

In the space provided below, construct your own outline of the chapter. Before you begin, refer to the "Key Topics" (section headings – above), introductory paragraph, chapter conclusion ("The First Cities: What Difference Do They Make"?) and "Review Questions" to help you identify the major questions and issues covered in the chapter and the author's main arguments and interpretations. This will aid you in deciding what to include in your outline notes.

TRUE/FALSE QUESTIONS: Read each question carefully (answers at end of chapter).

1. Languages such as Chinese employ pictograms (a.k.a. pictographs), which are pictorial symbols representing an object or concept. ___
2. One of the chief features or characteristics that distinguished cities from agricultural villages was their much higher degree of occupational specialization. ___
3. *Quipu* were early versions of ceremonial temples in Peru, similar to Sumerian ziggurats. ___
4. "The Fertile Crescent" is an alternative name for Mesopotamia, the "land between the (Tigris and Euphrates) rivers, located in modern day Iraq. ___
5. The biblical "Tower of Babel" in Genesis probably refers to a Sumerian ziggurat. ___
6. The *Epic of Gilgamesh* details the Babylonian conquest of the Sumerian city-state of Uruk, the ruins of which can be found in modern day Iraq. ___
7. Examples of cuneiform writing can be found preserved on clay tablets, bas reliefs and ceremonial stele, or stone pillars, such as those used to display and publicize Hammurabi's law code. ___
8. Historians have cited the development of class and gender inequalities as two side-effects of the process of urbanization. ___
9. The term "city-state" refers to a form of political organization in which loyalty and obedience to a specific city and its laws, rather than to a nation, a single ruler, or a specific religion, was the primary source of identity. ___
10. Unlike Hammurabi or Sargon of Akkad, Gilgamesh of Uruk may have been a mythical figure. ___

MULTIPLE CHOICE: Select the response that completes the sentence or answers the question best.

1. Which of the following was <u>not</u> a factor in determining punishment, compensation, or behavioral restraints in the Law Code of Hammurabi?
    a. Gender
    b. Religion
    c. Social class
    d. Slave status

2. While early cities served many functions, archaeological excavations of Sumerian cities have led most scholars to agree that their primary function was as:
    a. Defensive fortresses
    b. Royal palaces
    c. Marketplaces
    d. Religious centers

3. The oldest known agricultural villages developed during the:
    a. Neolithic Age, in Mesopotamia
    b. Paleolithic Age, in the Great Rift Valley
    c. Ice Age, in northern China
    d. Mesolithic Age, in the Nile Valley

4. Archaeologists often refer to different Neolithic eras, regions and peoples by descriptions of their distinctive:
    a. Agricultural crops
    b. Stone tools
    c. Ziggurats, or temples
    d. Clay pottery

5. Which of the following conditions was apparently typical of the earliest cities and city-states:
    a. The existence of large numbers of slaves
    b. Destructive warfare with neighboring city-states
    c. The subordination of women to male dominance
    d. All of the above

6. The Sumerian *Epic of Gilgamesh* provides us with a superb depiction of:
   a. The all-powerful nature of Sumerian kingship
   b. A world in which humans were subject to the whims of powerful gods
   c. A society of unequal social classes
   d. The transition from agricultural village to city-state

7. The development of writing began with pictograms and culminated in:
   a. Ideograms
   b. Cuneiform writing
   c. Phonetic alphabets
   d. *Quipu*

8. In order to maintain order, organize public works and secure obedience to the rulers, city-states had to develop a new "civic loyalty," based upon the individual's identification with:
   a. Shared geographical space
   b. Ties of blood and kinship
   c. His or her social class
   d. All of the above

9. Which of the following areas has <u>not</u> been identified as an area of "innovative primary urbanization" – that is, a region in which cities developed independently, without benefiting from cultural diffusion from other areas?
   a. The Indus River valley, in modern-day Pakistan
   b. The Andes Mountains, in Peru
   c. The Niger River valley, in west Africa
   d. The mainland and islands of Greece

10. The wealth and semi-divine nature of Sumerian kings has been confirmed by the unearthing of:
   a. The ziggurat at Ur
   b. The Royal Standard of Ur
   c. Bas-reliefs
   d. The royal tombs of Ur

11. Among the many important inventions which the Sumerians appear to have developed are cuneiform script, the wheeled cart, irrigation systems and:
   a. The brewing of ale
   b. The manufacture of paper
   c. Slash and burn agriculture
   d. All of the above

12. The Jomon people of Japan were a particularly distinctive village society because:
   a. They produced the first known examples of clay pottery.
   b. Their permanent village settlements were <u>not</u> based on agriculture.
   c. Their culture spread throughout Japan.
   d. They were peaceful agriculturalists.

13. Considerable architectural and literary evidence exists that suggests the wealthiest and most powerful class in the cities of ancient Sumer may have been the:
   a. Kings
   b. Soldiers
   c. Priests
   d. Scribes

14. The various Sumerian city-states seem to have warred with each other frequently, which rendered them vulnerable to conquest from outside, by:
    a. Sargon of Akkad and Gilgamesh of Uruk
    b. Gilgamesh of Uruk and Hammurabi of Babylon
    c. Ashurbanipal of Assyria and Gilgamesh of Uruk
    d. Sargon of Akkad and Hammurabi of Babylon

15. The larger cities of Mesopotamia attained a size of approximately 1½ sq. mi. in area and a population of:
    a. 5,000
    b. 35,000-50,000
    c. 350,000-500,000
    d. 5,000,000

MAP ANALYSIS: The following exercises are based on the maps on pp. 45, 46, 47, and 52 of the text. Use the outline map on the next page to complete the questions.

1. Using the map ("The spread of civilizations") on p. 47, locate and label the five river valleys in the eastern hemisphere in which "innovative primary urbanization" occurred between 3300 B.C.E. and 400 C.E.

2. Using all the maps in "Turning Point: The Agricultural Village" and Chapter 2, locate and label the following:
    a. Jericho
    b. Ban Po
    c. the Fertile Crescent
    d. the Niger River
    e. Mesoamerica
    f. Zimbabwe
    g. Babylon
    h. Anasazi Pueblo society
    i. the principal Mesopotamian trade routes
    j. Ur

3. Using the map ("The origins of agriculture and domestic animals") on p. 41, locate and identify the areas that produced each of the following crops or domesticated animals: rice, tubers, sheep, wheat, llamas and maize.

4. Studying all five maps in the chapter and considering the relative locations of the five core areas of urbanization and their proximity to one another, what inferences might be made regarding their influence on each other and on nearby "core areas of subsequent development"?

STUDY QUESTIONS

Consider each of the following questions carefully. Be prepared to supply specific evidence and examples to support your points in a class discussion or concise, well-organized written essay.

1. Describe and compare the distinctive attributes of early cities with those of agricultural villages, with regards to size, function, occupations, social hierarchy and political organization.

2. Although cities fostered enormous strides in human progress – writing systems, architecture, irrigation technology, art, literature and trade, for example – a number of commentators have also pointed out a darker side to urbanization and its effects. In short, cities may not have been an unmixed blessing to humankind. Discuss some of the "nasty side-effects" of urbanization, citing specific examples from the reading.

3. Research among surviving hunter-gatherer peoples suggests that they work less hard, enjoy more free time and are generally happier, healthier and better-adjusted than the evidence would suggest concerning early agricultural peoples. Given this fact, why might hunter-gatherer peoples have begun to settle down into the mundane, laborious existence of village farmers?

HOW DO WE KNOW?

The following questions are based on the various illustrations or quotations and extracts from primary source documents and historical interpretations in the chapter.

1. Using the *Code of Hammurabi* (p. 59) as your only source at first, make as many inferences as you can about the society of ancient Mesopotamia as you can from the actual evidence. Which of those inferences can be supported or corroborated by <u>other</u> primary sources reproduced or described in the text?

2. Using the *Epic of Gilgamesh* (p. 57) as your only source at first, repeat the same exercise as required in the previous question.

3. Spodek discusses modern critiques of urbanization by Karl Marx, Lewis Mumford and Gerda Lerner on p. 60. What evidence can you find to support their respective critiques in the various documents and other primary sources reproduced in the chapter?

TRUE/FALSE ANSWERS: 1-F; 2-T; 3-F; 4-F; 5-T; 6-F; 7-T; 8-T; 9-T; 10-T

MULTIPLE CHOICE ANSWERS: 1-B; 2-D; 3-A; 4-D; 5-D; 6-B; 7-C; 8-A; 9-D; 10-D; 11-A; 12-B; 13-C; 14-D; 15-B

3   RIVER VALLEY CIVILIZATIONS

THE NILE AND THE INDUS, 7000 B.C.E. – 750 B.C.E.

KEY TOPICS
- **Egypt: the Gift of the Nile**
- **The Indus Valley Civilization and its Mysteries**

CHAPTER NOTES

     In the space provided below, construct your own outline of the chapter. Before you begin, refer to the "Key Topics" (section headings – above), introductory paragraph, chapter conclusion ("The Cities of the Nile and the Indus: What Difference Do They Make"?) and "Review Questions" to help you identify the major questions and issues covered in the chapter and the author's main arguments and interpretations. This will aid you in deciding what to include in your outline notes.

TRUE/FALSE QUESTIONS: Read each question carefully (answers at end of chapter).

1) Cities of the Indus Valley civilization exhibited a high degree of urban planning; and featured such amenities as wide streets, bath houses, underground sewerage systems, and different residential areas for different occupational groups. ___
2) The pharaoh Amenhotep IV challenged the religious order of ancient Egypt by rejecting polytheism (the worship of many gods) in favor of one, the sun god Amon. ___
3) Mass migrations or invasions by Aryan peoples from the north completely obliterated the flourishing Indus Valley civilization sometime around 1500 B.C.E., leaving only archeological traces. ___
4) Egypt has been called "the Gift of the Nile" because the river's great length and predictable flooding provided an abundance of fresh water and nutrient-rich silt for agriculture. ___
5) The writing of ancient Harappan civilization was successfully deciphered after the British discovery of the Rosetta Stone in 1858. ___
6) Unlike Sumerian cuneiform writing, which was done on clay tablets, Egyptian hieroglyphics were written on sheets of papyrus, a paper-like material made from reeds. ___
7) The Egyptian state developed more centralized organization and power during the Middle Kingdom, ca. 2050-1750 B.C.E. ___
8) *Nomes* were regional temple complexes situated at regular intervals along the Nile. ___
9) Unlike cities in Mesopotamia or the Indus Valley civilizations, Egyptian cities were not "city-states" and generally served only one principal purpose each, either as religious centers, trading ports, or administrative centers. ___
10) Most of ancient Egypt's most famous monumental architecture, such as the Sphinx and Pyramids at Giza, are relics of the Middle Kingdom. ___

MULTIPLE CHOICE: Select the response that completes the sentence or answers the question best.

1. Archaeological excavations of many Egyptian and Harappan sites have reached the limits of their usefulness because:
   a. Looters have stolen so many artifacts over the years
   b. Later cities have been built over ancient sites
   c. The high water table has eroded many subterranean structures
   d. All of the above

2. Modern Egyptology began with the:
   a. French invasion of Egypt in 1798
   b. Building of the Suez Canal in the 1860's
   c. British occupation of Egypt in 1882
   d. German invasion of Egypt in 1942

3. The <u>most</u> serious obstacle to modern understanding of the Indus Valley civilization has been the:
   a. Destruction of much Harappan material culture by the Aryan invaders of India, c. 1500 B.C.E.
   b. Absence of decipherable written records
   c. Submergence of many Harappan sites by rising water tables
   d. Use of bricks and rubble from many sites by British railway builders in 19th century India

4. For most of its long history, ancient Egyptian religion was characterized by the worship of a pantheon of god and goddesses, except during the reign of the pharoah _____ in the period of the New Kingdom.
   a. Khufu
   b. Narmer (or Menes)
   c. Djoser
   d. Akhenaten

5. Egyptian legends, which may or may not be correct, attribute the formation of the unification of Upper and Lower Egypt to the early king:
   a. Khufu
   b. Narmer (or Menes)
   c. Djoser
   d. Akhenaten

6. One of the earliest monumental tomb structures – a precursor of the great pyramids – was the *mastaba* of the king:
   a. Khufu
   b. Narmer (or Menes)
   c. Djoser
   d. Akhenaten

7. Archaeologists have been especially impressed by the creation of which sort of art by Harappan sculpture:
   a. Depictions of the human body and body movement
   b. Statues of gods and goddesses
   c. Monuments on royal tombs
   d. All of the above

8. Osiris, father of Horus and husband-brother of Isis, was one of the most important Egyptian gods, because he represented:
   a. Fertility
   b. Wisdom
   c. Order
   d. The sun

9. The increase in monumental tombs and funerary objects during the Old Kingdom in Egypt has been associated with which of the following by archaeologists?
   a. Monotheism (worship of a single god)
   b. State-building
   c. An increase in trade
   d. All of the above

10. Traces of urban settlements in the Indus Valley date from as early as _____ B.C.E., making it older than Egyptian civilization.
    a. 1,500
    b. 3,500
    c. 7,000
    d. 10,000

11. Evidence for the date of the earliest Indus Valley urban settlements comes from excavations at a site near:
    a. Harappa
    b. Kalibangan
    c. Mohenjo-Daro
    d. Mehrgarh

12. Which of the following information can be inferred from written sources by archaeologists?
    a. Information about the nature of a people's values and religious beliefs
    b. Information about the nature of a civilization's trade and economy
    c. Information about a society's state and political institutions
    d. All of the above

13. Which of the following is <u>not</u> known with any degree of certainty about Indus Valley civilization?
    a. The names and identity of its rulers
    b. The reasons for its decline and fall
    c. The degree of political independence of its cities
    d. All of the above

14. Which of the following is <u>not</u> known with any degree of certainty about Egyptian civilization?
    a. The names and identity of its rulers
    b. The reasons for its decline and fall
    c. The date and circumstances of its unification
    d. All of the above

15. Important trade products of Harappan civilization included ceramic pottery, statuettes, beaded bronze jewelry and:
    a. Cotton textiles
    b. Rice
    c. Silk textiles
    d. Iron weapons and tools

MAP ANALYSIS: (The following questions are based on the maps on pp. 52, 67, and 81.)

1. Using the maps on pp. 67 and 81 ("Cities of the Indus" – top), compare the extent, concentration and topography (physical features) of Egyptian and Indus Valley civilizations. What inferences can perhaps be made – or corroborated – about their respective societies, economies and states?

2. What can be inferred regarding interaction among Egyptian, Indus Valley and Mesopotamian civilizations from the map ("Mesopotamian trade") on p. 52? What goods were produced in each area and traded to the others? What other areas were involved in this trade?

3. On the outline map of Egypt on the next page, locate and identify the places identified with the following:
    a. The pharaoh Akhenaten
    b. The Great Sphinx and the Pyramid of Khefren
    c. The approximate boundary between Upper and Lower Egypt (label each)
    d. The boundary between Egypt and Nubia

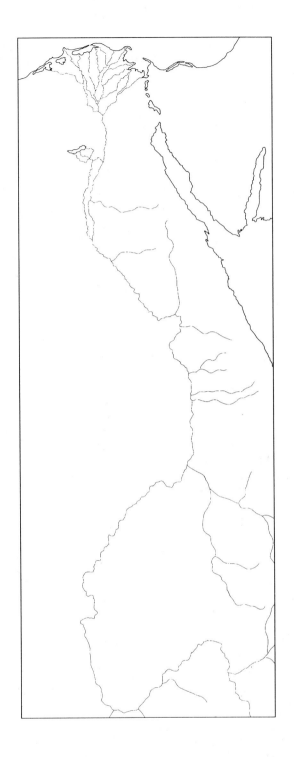

STUDY QUESTIONS: Consider each of the following questions carefully. Be prepared to supply specific evidence and examples to support your points in a class discussion or concise, well-organized essay.

1. Discuss the academic debate on the interaction between the Harappan, or Indus Valley civilization and the nomadic Aryan invaders. What did scholars previously think happened to the cities of the Indus Valley. Why? What is the current opinion on the interchange between the two peoples and the "legacy of the Indus" civilization? What sort of evidence is it based upon?

2. Citing specific examples, compare the relationship between the growth and relative importance of individual cities and the development of the state in the three river valley civilizations surveyed thus far: Mesopotamia, Egypt and the Indus Valley. In which civilization were cities most important? Least?

3. How do archaeologists and geographers explain the establishment and growth of towns and cities along the Nile? Citing specific examples, explain the different primary purposes which seem to have been served by Egyptian cities.

HOW DO WE KNOW?

The following questions are based on the various illustrations or quotations and extracts from primary source documents and historical interpretations in the text.

1. What can we infer about both daily life and concepts of the afterlife in ancient Egypt from the monumental tomb structures such as the Great Pyramid of Khufu at Giza or the *mastaba* of Djoser at Saqqara and their contents? What would have been required for the construction of such monuments? Why would they have been built?

2. How do the physical layout and the design of various buildings at Mohenjo-Daro compare with those at Egyptian sites? What have some archaeologists inferred about the nature of Indus Valley civilization from these differences?

3. Written sources are very abundant for ancient Egypt after, c. 2300 B.C.E., and provide archaeologists with a wealth of information about the civilization that cannot be easily inferred from artifacts and buildings. Using the two extracts from ancient Egypt reprinted on pp. 76-77 of the text ("The Story of Si-nuhe" and the *Book of the Dead*), what inferences might be made about Egyptian society?

4. Construct a comparative chart presenting what you have learned about the geography, social structure, cities, religion, government, economic life and standard of living of ancient Mesopotamia, Egypt and the Indus Valley using <u>only</u> the various primary sources (documents, photographs, diagrams) at your disposal in Chapters 2 and 3.

TRUE/FALSE ANSWERS: 1-T; 2-F; 3-F; 4-T; 5-F; 6-T; 7-T; 8-F; 9-T; 10-T

MULTIPLE CHOICE ANSWERS: 1-D; 2-A; 3-B; 4-D; 5-B; 6-C; 7-A; 8-C; 9-B; 10-C; 11-D; 12-D; 13-D; 14-C; 15-A

4   A POLYCENTRIC WORLD

CITIES AND STATES IN EAST ASIA, THE AMERICAS, AND WEST AFRICA, 1700 B.C.E. – 1000 C.E.

KEY TOPICS:

- **China: The Xia, Shang and Zhou Dynasties**
- **The Western Hemisphere: Mesoamerica and South America**
- **West Africa: The Niger River Valley**

CHAPTER NOTES

      In the space provided below, construct your own outline of the chapter. Before you begin, refer to the "Key Topics" (section headings – above), introductory paragraph, chapter conclusion ("The First Cities: What Difference Do They Make"?) and "Review Questions" to help you identify the major questions and issues covered in the chapter and the author's main arguments and interpretations. This will aid you in deciding what to include in your outline notes.

TRUE/FALSE QUESTIONS: Read each question carefully (answers at end of chapter).

1) *Chinampas*, the artificial fields constructed out of natural swampland, were characteristic features of many different early Mesoamerican societies, beginning before the Olmecs. ___
2) According to archeologist Paul Wheatley, evidence such as oracle bones and human skeletal remains at sites such as Anyang suggest that the earliest Chinese cities served mainly as trading centers. ___
3) Although much smaller in their dimensions, the Pyramids of the Sun and the Moon at Teotihuacán in the Valley of Mexico appear to have served the same functions as those at Giza in Egypt. ___
4) Archeologists and historians now believe that the Xia dynasty existed only in Chinese myths. ___
5) Owing to the unpredictable nature of the Yellow River, one of the most important functions of early Chinese governments was flood control. ___
6) Today it is generally accepted by archeologists and historians that the peoples of West Africa, like those of Western Europe, learned the various arts of urbanization through trade with others. ___
7) Like the Mayan civilization in Mesoamerica, Inca civilization in South America was based on earlier urban civilizations in its region and owed much to its predecessors. ___
8) The Niger River valley civilization differed from others we have studied so far, in that the usual traits of extreme social hierarchy and governmental centralization may not have been present. ___
9) The "Mandate of Heaven" refers to the "cosmo-magical" nature of many early cities in China. ___
10) The Bantu were a people who, starting from their indigenous beginnings in the lower Niger River Valley, migrated throughout northern and western Africa between 500 B.C.E and 500 C.E. ___

MULTIPLE CHOICE: Select the response that completes the sentence or answers the question best.

1. The Bantu peoples of the lower Niger Valley exerted enormous influence on African development through:
   a. Establishment of a great trading kingdom in west Africa
   b. Lifelike terra-cotta sculptures of animals and humans
   c. Migrations throughout sub-Saharan Africa
   d. Adoption of the Islamic religion

2. A major reason for the shifting of capital cities in early Chinese dynasties was:
   a. Destruction caused by the flooding of the Huang He (Yellow River)
   b. Warfare between neighboring states
   c. The "cosmo-magical" functions of the cities
   d. All of the above

3. Which of the following sets of crops describe the agricultural staples of American civilizations?
   a. Cotton, rice, and kola nuts
   b. Cotton, maize, and dates
   c. Rice, millet and root crops
   d. Cotton, maize, root crops

4. Archaeologists believe the core areas of South American urbanization were located in:
   a. The Andes Mountains
   b. The Valley of Mexico
   c. The Yucatan Peninsula
   d. The coastal plain of Peru

5. One modern archaeologist has argued that the Niger Valley city of Jenne-jeno:
   a. Functioned primarily a religious shrine center
   b. Developed as a response to Muslim traders crossing the Sahara
   c. Pre-dated trans-Saharan trade with the Muslims of North Africa
   d. Was the capital of a centralized state

6. Mayan hieroglyphics were finally deciphered:
   a. By matching them against the Latin and Spanish texts of the *Popul Vuh*
   b. Through linguistic analysis of the structure of the writing
   c. With the help of surviving descendants of the Maya
   d. All of the above

7. Mayan and Aztec civilizations fought frequent wars for the principal purpose of:
    a. Controlling trade routes to the coastal areas
    b. Capturing prisoners for human sacrifices to the gods
    c. Controlling sources of water
    d. Acquiring territory for royal relatives to rule

8. A major difference between early urban civilizations in the Americas and those in Asia and Africa was:
    a. The later development of agriculture in the Americas
    b. The absence of metal tools and weapons in the Americas
    c. A less stratified social structure in the Americas
    d. The lack of any system of writing in the Americas

9. It appears that, after an early Chinese dynasty was superseded by a rival, the defeated state:
    a. Was totally incorporated into the new dynasty
    b. Was utterly destroyed by the new dynasty
    c. Continued to exist, but with reduced power and territory
    d. Was given to a member of the new dynasty to rule

10. Which of the following is perhaps the most characteristic monumental art of the Olmec civilization?
    a. The Pyramid of the Sun at Teotihuacán
    b. The royal tombs at Sipan
    c. The huge pebble-drawings in the desert at Nazca
    d. The giant stone head carvings at San Lorenzo and La Venta

11. Until the 1970s, scholars generally discounted the possibility of primary urbanization in Africa because:
    a. Early African agricultural societies had no written language
    b. Early African cities were thought to have developed as responses to outside influences
    c. The cities of west Africa were primarily trading centers, rather than "cosmo-magical" sites
    d. Early African agricultural societies had no metal tools or weapons

12. Based on the evidence presented in this chapter, which of the following civilizations was the only one that did not practice ritual human sacrifice?
    a. Mayan civilization in Mesoamerica
    b. Jenne-Jenno in West Africa
    c. Shang Dynasty China
    d. Moche civilization in South America

13. The "classic phase" of Mayan civilization occurred closest in time to which of the following?
    a. The Zhou Dynasty in China
    b. The peak of the power of Teotihuacan in Mesoamerica
    c. The formation of the west African trading kingdom of Ghana
    d. The rise of the Inca Empire in South America

14. 20th century archaeological excavations have tended to confirm the veracity of the work of this Chinese court historian who lived from 140-87 B.C.E.
    a. Dung Zobin
    b. Lady Hao
    c. Sima Qian
    d. Confucius

15. In southern Africa, great walled structures called _____ enclosed local royal rulers who maintained extensive contact with Indian Ocean traders.
    a. *chinampas*
    b. *zimbabwes*
    c. *pueblos*
    d. *shamans*

MAP ANALYSIS

1. Using the maps on pp. 112 and 113, locate and identify the following on the outline map below:
   a. The cities of Jenne, Benin and Timbuktu
   b. Two major west African trading states
   c. The homeland of the Nok people
   d. Major trade routes across the Sahara Desert
   e. The areas settled by Bantu-speaking peoples

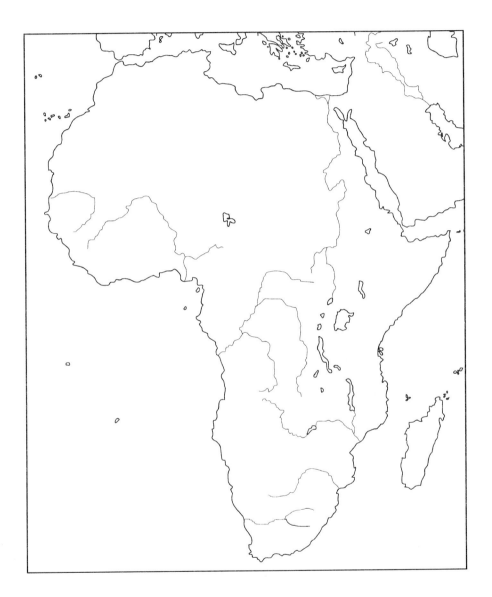

2. Using the text and the maps on p. 99, locate and identify the following on the outline map below:
   a. The city-state ruled by King Great-Jaguar-Paw
   b. The civilization that built the royal tombs at Sipan
   c. The largest pre-Aztec city in the Americas
   d. The extent of Mayan civilization
   e. The Andes Mountains
   f. The Mesoamerican civilization centered around La Venta and San Lorenzo
   g. The extent of the largest empire in South America

STUDY QUESTIONS: Consider each of the following questions carefully. Be prepared to supply specific evidence and examples to support your points in a class discussion or a concise, well-organized essay.

1. In the three chapters in Part 2 ("Settling Down") Howard Spodek posits a cross-cultural model of urban development and seeks to apply it to seven different civilizations. What are the basic elements of this model? Citing specific evidence from the primary sources presented in each chapter, to what extent do the urban settlements in each of the civilizations reviewed conform to that model?

2. Describe the powers, responsibilities and functions of Xia, Shang, and Chou dynasty rulers. How did they attain their positions? What was expected from them by their subjects? How would the term "cosmo-magical" be applied to them? What about the term "Mandate of Heaven"?

3. What are the two principal questions regarding the origins and functions of Jenne-jeno and other early Niger Valley settlements? How do these questions illustrate the outlines of the historical controversy relating to urban development in West Africa?

HOW DO WE KNOW?

The following questions are based on the various illustrations or quotations and extracts from primary source documents and historical interpretations in the chapter.

1. What is meant by the term "cosmo-magical cities" coined by the geographer and anthropologist Paul Wheatley? What sorts of archeological evidence have been found in the various urban civilizations discussed in this chapter which would support his argument? Be sure to include specific examples from China, the Americas and Africa.

2. Compare the Mayan creation myth related in the *Popul Vuh* with the Hebrew creation myth found in the book of *Genesis*, the Indian creation myth in the *Rigveda* and the Akkadian *Enuma Elish* (pp. 5-6). In what respects are they similar? Different? What does each myth reveal about its culture's concepts of the relationship between humans and their gods or God?

3. The relationship of cities and state formation is one of the themes of this chapter. Citing specific examples from the text, illustrations and primary source documents, demonstrate which of the urban civilizations discussed in the chapter were centers of centralized political states and which were not. What types of evidence seem to be most indicative of larger state formations?

TRUE/FALSE ANSWERS: 1-T; 2-F; 3-F; 4-F; 5-T; 6-F; 7-T; 8-T; 9-F; 10-F

MULTIPLE CHOICE ANSWERS: 1-C; 2-B; 3-D; 4-A; 5-C; 6-B; 7-B; 8-B; 9-C; 10-D; 11-B; 12-B; 13-B; 14-C; 15-B

5   DAWN OF THE EMPIRES

EMPIRE-BUILDING IN NORTH AFRICA, WEST ASIA, AND THE MEDITERRANEAN, 2000 B.C.E. – 300 B.C.E.

KEY TOPICS
- **The Meaning of Empire**
- **The Earliest Empires**
- **The Persian Empire**
- **The Greek City-States**
- **The Empire of Alexander the Great**

CHAPTER NOTES

In the space provided below, construct your own outline of the chapter. Before you begin, refer to the "Key Topics" (section headings – above), introductory paragraph, chapter conclusion ("Empire Building: What Difference Does It Make"?) and "Review Questions" to help you identify the major questions and issues covered in the chapter and the author's main arguments and interpretations. This will aid you in deciding what to include in your outline notes.

TRUE/FALSE QUESTIONS: Read each question carefully (answers at end of chapter).

1) The term "Hellenism" refers to the culture of the city-states of Classical Greece. ___
2) The Hoplites, an Indo-European cultural group, successfully established an Empire in what is now Turkey with the aid of iron weapons and war chariots. ___
3) Sargon of Akkad established the first Mesopotamian empire in the middle of the 24th Century B.C.E. ___
4) New Kingdom Egypt exhibited both forms of imperial rule – dominance and hegemony – in its methods of ruling over its imperial conquests in Nubia and Palestine. ___
5) The last Achaemenid ruler of the Persian Empire was Cyrus the Great, whose armies were defeated in several battles by Alexander. ___
6) In all likelihood, the Minoan civilization on Crete was destroyed by a massive volcanic eruption around the year 1625 B.C.E. ___
7) During the Peloponnesian War, support for Sparta against Athens among Greek city-states was fueled by resentment of Athenian imperial policies and actions, including the destruction of the island state of Melos in 415 B.C.E. ___
8) *Oedipus Rex,* by Socrates, is perhaps the most famous tragedy written by an Athenian. ___
9) Unlike his philosophical mentor Plato, Aristotle argued for the political and social equality of women in Athenian society. ___
10) Under Darius I, the Persian Empire stretched from Macedonia in Greece to the Indus River valley in India. ___

MULTIPLE CHOICE: Select the response which completes the sentence or answers the question best.

1. In choosing to extend imperial rule to much of the known world of the time, Alexander the Great disregarded the arguments in favor of the small, self-governing *polis* that had been written by his own tutor, the Greek philosopher:
    a. Plato
    b. Pericles
    c. Aristotle
    d. Socrates

2. The Medes and Persians, who coalesced to form the Persian Empire, were both peoples of which of the following language-culture group?
    a. Semitic (Assyrian)
    b. Hittite
    c. Amorite
    d. Indo-European

3. The 19th century archaeological discoveries of the German scholar Heinrich Schliemann confirmed the historical existence of the Greek city-states of Mycenae and Troy, whose 10-year war had been related in:
    a. Plato's *Republic*
    b. Homer's *Iliad*
    c. Herodotus' *Persian Wars*
    d. Thucydides' *History of the Peloponnesian War*

4. The practice of imperial "hegemony" is best illustrated by the policies and actions of:
    a. Cyrus the Great of Persia
    b. Sargon of Akkad
    c. Ashurbanipal of Assyria
    d. Pericles of Athens

5. Based on the evidence from archaeological sources, it is now believed that the ethnic composition of ancient Egypt was predominantly:
    a. Semitic
    b. Mediterranean
    c. Nubian
    d. A mixture of all of the above

6. The political reforms of Solon and Cleisthenes aimed at creating an Athenian *polis* in which participation was <u>not</u> dependent upon:
   a. Gender
   b. Social class
   c. Residence in a *deme*
   d. Property ownership

7. The Peloponnesian War (435-401 B.C.E.) was caused by which of the following?
   a. Sparta's attempt to dominate Greece
   b. Persia's attempt to conquer Greece
   c. Athens' attempt to dominate Greece
   d. Macedonia's attempt to conquer Greece

8. Which of the following might be cited as a reason for the decline and fall of the Persian Empire?
   a. Failure of leadership
   b. Overextension of the administration
   c. Military defeat
   d. All of the above

9. The size of Greek city-states was determined in large measure by:
   a. Their popular assemblies
   b. The political theories of Aristotle
   c. The geography of Greece
   d. Persian control

10. The Egyptian New Kingdom reached its greatest extent of imperial control during the reign of the Pharoah:
    a. Rameses II
    b. Akhenaton
    c. Ptolemy
    d. Thutmosis I

11. According to Plato's *Republic*, the ideal state would be one administered by:
    a. A council of 400 male citizens
    b. A council of 500 male and female citizens
    c. A "philosopher-king" who would know what was best for all citizens
    d. Philip of Macedonia

12. Which of the following was <u>not</u> an accomplishment of Darius I of Persia?
    a. The conquest of Media, Babylonia, and Lydia
    b. The creation of units of local government called satrapies
    c. The building of the "Royal Road" from Susa to Sardis
    d. The construction of a canal linking the Nile River to the Red Sea

13. As an imperial ruler, Alexander the Great generally pursued a policy that could be described as:
    a. Ecumenicism
    b. Hegemony
    c. Dominance
    d. Realpolitik

14. Based on the primary source excerpts in the text, which of the following Athenians advocates a vision of a democratic state with which most Americans could identify?
    a. Socrates
    b. Plato
    c. Pericles
    d. Aristotle

15. According to Spodek, which of the following was <u>not</u> necessarily an attribute of early empires?
   a. A single system of coinage
   b. A single administrative language
   c. An efficient tax system
   d. A single state religion

MAP ANALYSIS

A. The exercises below should be answered by referring to the map ("Classical Greece") on p. 152 of the text.

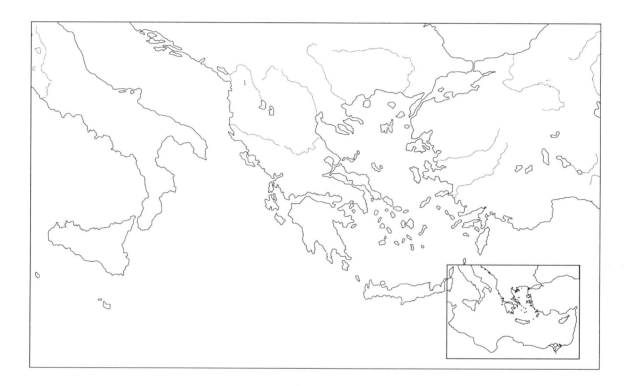

1. Using the maps pp. 135 & 152 for reference, locate and identify the following: Knossos, Troy, Athens, Sparta, Marathon, Thermopylae, Melos, Syracuse, Macedonia, Anatolia, Crete, and the Mediterranean, Ionian and Aegean Seas. Shade in the areas which were incorporated into the Persian Empire.

2. Explain how Greek geography and topography influenced the development of the *polis* and the history of classical Greece? Cite specific evidence from the map.

B. The exercises below should be completed using the maps on pp. 127, 129, 133, 135, and 154 in the text.

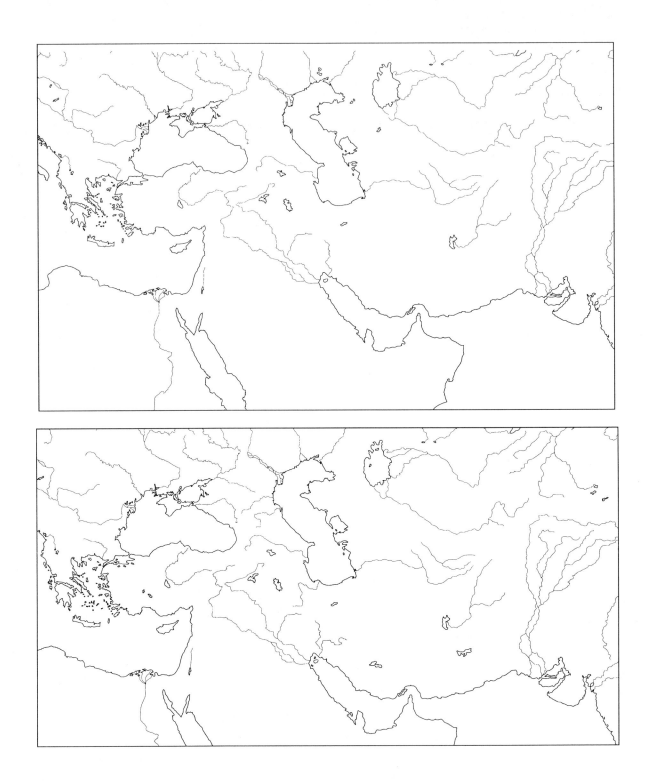

3. On the maps on the previous page, superimpose the outlines of the boundaries of the following empires in different color pencils: Akkad (Agade), the Egyptian New Kingdom, the Hittites, Assyria, Achaemenid Persia, and Alexander the Great. Locate, identify and label the capitals of each of these empires.

4. Looking at your completed maps, explain the reasons why the conquests of Alexander the Great are considered to have laid the foundations for a Hellenistic cultural ecumene. What is an "ecumene"? What various elements would have been included in the "Hellenistic cultural ecumene"?

STUDY QUESTIONS: Consider each of the following questions carefully. Be prepared to supply specific evidence and examples to support your points in a class discussion or concise, well-organized written essay.

1. List and explain the various attributes shared by all the major empires surveyed in this chapter, citing specific examples from at least three different empires.

2. Define and explain the terms "hegemony" and "dominance" as they relate to methods of imperial rule. Based on the available evidence, how would the Assyrian, Persian, Athenian and Macedonian empires be classified? Support your assertions with specific examples and evidence.

3. In the chapter introduction, the author cites five common reasons for imperial decline and dissolution. Which of these can be assigned to the various empires discussed in the chapter? Again, furnish specific examples to support your argument.

HOW DO WE KNOW?

The following questions are based on the various illustrations or quotations and extracts from primary sources and historical interpretations in the chapter.

1. What was the relationship between the citizens and the *polis* (city-state) in Athens? Who <u>were</u> the "citizens"? In what respects was Athens <u>less</u> democratic than modern democracies? In what respects was it perhaps <u>more</u> democratic? Cite specific evidence from primary sources, archaeology and historical arguments to support your answer.

2. Discuss the attitudes towards and status of women in classical Athens, as revealed by contemporary Greek sources and modern historians. What characteristics of the Greek value system and the society of the Athenian *polis* might account for the prevailing view of women's roles at the time? Cite evidence from as many different sources as you can.

3. Compare the values of pre-classical Greece, as reflected in the archaeological evidence from Minoan and Mycenean civilization and from Homer's *Iliad* and *Odyssey*, with the values of classical Athens, as reflected in the works of Thucydides and Plato and classical Athenian art and drama. How are they similar? In what respects do they differ? How would you account for those differences?

TRUE/FALSE ANSWERS: 1-F; 2-F; 3-T; 4-T; 5-F; 6-F; 7-T; 8-F; 9-F; 10-T

MULTIPLE CHOICE ANSWERS: 1-C; 2-D; 3-B; 4-A; 5-D; 6-B; 7-C; 8-B; 9-C; 10-D; 11-C; 12-A; 13-B; 14-C; 15-D

6   ROME AND THE BARBARIANS
THE RISE AND FALL OF EMPIRE, 750 B.C.E. – 500 C.E.

KEY TOPICS
- **From Hill Town to Empire**
- **The Barbarians and the Fall of the Roman Empire**

CHAPTER NOTES

In the space provided below, construct your own outline of the chapter. Before you begin, refer to the "Key Topics" (section headings – above), introductory paragraph, chapter conclusion ("The Legacy of the Roman Empire: What Difference Does It Make"?) and "Review Questions" to help you identify the major questions and issues covered in the chapter and the author's main arguments and interpretations. This will aid you in deciding what to include in your outline notes.

TRUE/FALSE QUESTIONS: Read each question carefully (answers at end of chapter).

1) The History of Rome, like that of Athens, suggests that it is possible to be both a Republic and an Empire at the same time. ____
2) Of all the previous civilizations we have studied so far, Roman society and culture was probably most heavily influenced by that of ancient Troy. ____
3) It is really incorrect to say that the Roman Empire "fell" in the 4th Century C.E., since the eastern half of the empire survived for almost a thousand years afterwards. ____
4) The term "Punic Wars" refers to the policy of punishment that the Roman Republic followed against its Carthaginian enemy. ____
5) Although the Roman Emperor was considered a god and state rituals and sacrifices were offered to him, as well as the traditional pagan deities, Rome generally pursued a policy of religious toleration within its empire. ____
6) The Huns were a barbarian people who at different times threatened both China and Rome. ____
7) The term "bread and circuses" refers to the Roman policy of preventing open conflict between the rich and poor by providing free food and entertainment for the masses. ____
8) The Roman Empire reached its greatest territorial extent under Julius Caesar in 180 C.E. ____
9) The 18th Century English historian Edward Gibbon argued that Christianity was a major factor in the decline of the Roman Empire. ____
10) A major religious issue during the reign of the Byzantine Emperor Justinian was the controversy over the human versus divine nature of Christ. ____

MULTIPLE CHOICE: Select the response that completes the sentence or answers the question best.

1. Virgil's epic poem, the *Aeneid*, connects the founding of Rome with which of the following?
    a. The legend of Romulus and Remus and the she-wolf
    b. Ancient Greece and the Trojan War
    c. The Etruscans of northern Italy
    d. Celtic invasions of Italy

2. In what capacity did Hannibal play a significant role in Roman history?
    a. As the founder of the philosophy of Stoicism
    b. As the leader of the barbarian Huns
    c. As the emperor who built the first wall in northern Britain
    d. As a Carthaginian general who invaded Italy and nearly defeated Rome

3. Throughout the period of the Republic, the principal law-making body of Rome was:
    a. The tribunes of the plebeians
    b. The Roman senate
    c. The consuls and praetors
    d. The *jus gentium*

4. Roman control was made attractive to conquered peoples through:
    a. Grants of citizenship and the protection of Roman law
    b. The Roman policy of religious toleration
    c. The building of Roman towns, roads and aqueducts
    d. All of the above

5. The Roman statesman Cicero, philosopher Seneca, and emperor Marcus Aurelius were all followers of which Roman belief system?
    a. Emperor-god worship
    b. Stoicism
    c. Christianity
    d. Zoroastrianism

6. The Roman Republic was ended and the Roman Empire established by:
   a. Augustus Caesar
   b. Gaius Marius
   c. Julius Caesar
   d. Diocletian

7. The workings of the Roman "patron-client relationship" can be clearly seen in:
   a. The rights of the *paterfamilias*
   b. Relations between patricians and plebeians
   c. The loyalty of soldiers to their military commanders
   d. All of the above

8. The movement of Germanic tribes into the Roman Empire was hastened because they were being pushed westward by other people, known as:
   a. Celts
   b. Goths
   c. Gauls
   d. Huns

9. The Roman Empire reached the limits of its greatest extent under the Emperor:
   a. Claudius (51-54 C.E.)
   b. Trajan (98-117 C.E.)
   c. Caracalla (212-217 C.E.)
   d. Justinian (527-565 C.E.)

10. Which of the following policies was implemented by Caesar Augustus?
    a. The legalization of Christianity throughout the empire
    b. The extension of Roman citizenship to all residents of the empire
    c. The tightening of legal restrictions on Roman women
    d. The division of the empire into eastern and western halves

11. The word "barbarian" was used by the Romans to refer to peoples who were considered inferior because
    a. They did not speak Latin or Greek.
    b. They were nomadic herders, rather than settled farmers.
    c. They destroyed Roman cities.
    d. All of the above

12. The reforms of Gracchus were aimed primarily at:
    a. Giving political rights to the plebeian class in Rome
    b. Extending citizenship to Rome's Italian allies
    c. Providing poor relief and land to ex-soldiers
    d. Relieving the restrictions on Roman women

13. Christianity was established as a legal religion of the Roman Empire by the Emperor:
    a. Constantine
    b. Caracalla
    c. Marcus Aurelius
    d. Augustus

14. Which of the following actions exemplified the policy of the "New Wisdom"?
    a. The granting of citizenship rights to the people of all Rome's Italian allies
    b. The building of the *Hagia Sophia* cathedral in Constantinople
    c. The senate's recognition of the rights of the plebeians
    d. The destruction of the cities of Capua and Carthage

15. The transport of bulk items such as grain, olive oil, and leather, to Rome, was most often done:
    a. By camel, via caravans from Asia
    b. By slaves, via the network of Roman roads
    c. By ship, across the Mediterranean Sea
    d. By returning soldiers, who were required to bring the supplies back with them

MAP ANALYSIS

The following exercises are based on the maps on pp. 168, 183, 192, 195, and 197 in the text.

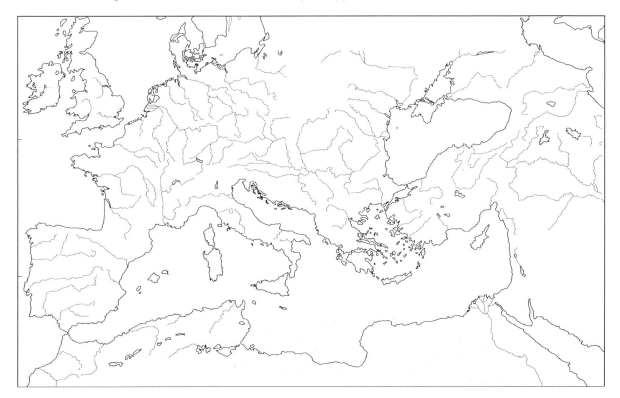

1. On the outline map above, locate and identify the following:
    a. The boundaries of the Roman Empire, c. 180 C.E.
    b. The cities of Rome, Carthage, Athens, Alexandria, Jerusalem, Pompeii, and Constantinople
    c. The Mediterranean, Aegean, Black and North Seas; and islands of Sicily, Crete and Britain
    d. The Tiber, Po, Rhine and Danube Rivers; and the Alps, Pyrenees and Atlas Mountains
    e. The migration routes of the various barbarian tribes
    f. The boundaries of the Byzantine Empire and the Germanic successor kingdoms

2. Considering your completed map, in what respects could the Roman Empire have served as a successor to and extension of the Hellenistic Ecumene? What were the effects on Rome's historical and cultural legacy?

STUDY QUESTIONS: Consider each of the following questions carefully. Be prepared to supply specific evidence and examples to support your points in a class discussion or concise, well-organized written essay.

1. The text argues that "the earliest enduring social structure in Rome was the patron-client relationship" (p. 170) and implies that, in different forms, it was perhaps the most important relationship in Roman society. What exactly was the nature of the "patron-client relationship"? What different forms did it assume in Roman society and politics and how did it affect the course of Roman history so profoundly?

2. Gaius Marius, the brothers Tiberius and Gaius Gracchus and the emperor Augustus Caesar are all presented as reformers in the text and all would certainly have viewed themselves as such. But it is arguable that their various reforms only made Rome's problems worse in the long run. First put these four "reformers" in the correct chronological order and then discuss this assertion, with particular reference to their respective policies.

3. Compare this chapter's account of the "Decline and Fall" of the Roman Empire with the general classification of causes of imperial decline enumerated in Chapter 5 (p. 123). Which of these general causes seem to have applied to Rome's decline? Which one, in your own view, was most important? Cite specific examples from Chapter 6 to support your argument.

HOW DO WE KNOW?

The following questions are based on the various illustrations or quotations and extracts from primary source documents and historical interpretations in the chapter.

1. How do we know what daily life was like in ancient Rome and the Roman Empire? What sources have been used by historians to make generalizations about the conditions of Roman material culture and living standards? What do those sources reveal? Cite specific evidence from the primary sources.

2. Discuss the development and status of Christianity in the Roman Empire. How was it spread so quickly throughout the Empire? Why were Christians persecuted, in contrast to the Romans' usual policy of religious toleration? How did it eventually become the dominant religion? What role might it have played in the decline of the empire?

3. What and who were the "Barbarians?" How "barbarian" were they? What do we know about them and from what sources? Exactly how did they contribute to the decline of the Roman Empire, according to the chapter?

TRUE/FALSE ANSWERS: 1-T; 2-F; 3-T; 4-F; 5-T; 6-T; 7-T; 8-F; 9-T; 10-T

MULTIPLE CHOICE ANSWERS: 1-B; 2-D; 3-C; 4-D; 5-B; 6-A; 7-D; 8-D; 9-B; 10-C; 11-A; 12-C; 13-A; 14-D; 15-C

7 CHINA

FRACTURE AND UNIFICATION: THE QIN, HAN, SUI AND TANG DYNASTIES, 200 B.C.E. – 900 C.E.

KEY TOPICS
- **The Qin Dynasty**
- **The Han Dynasty**
- **Disintegration and Reunification**
- **Imperial China**

CHAPTER NOTES

In the space provided below, construct your own outline of the chapter. Before you begin, refer to the "Key Topics" (section headings – above), introductory paragraph, chapter conclusion ("Legacies for the Future: What Difference Do They Make"?) and "Review Questions" to help you identify the major questions and issues covered in the chapter and the author's main arguments and interpretations. This will aid you in deciding what to include in your outline notes.

TRUE/FALSE QUESTIONS: Read each question carefully (answers at end of chapter).

1) Unlike Confucianism, which revered formal education and scholarship, Daoists believed that simplicity, spontaneity, and mysticism were superior approached to life. ___
2) The term "sinicization" refers to the military conquest of foreign peoples by the Chinese. ___
3) The female moralist Ban Zhao sought to apply Confucian principles to gender relations in China. ___
4) The Trung Sisters might be cited as good examples of Ban Zhao's "Admonitions to Women." ___
5) Confucianism was first adopted as a Chinese state philosophy under the Qin Dynasty. ___
6) The planning and construction of the Japanese city of Nara could be considered a perfect example of "sinicization" in practice. ___
7) One of the cultural side-effects of the decline and fall of the Han Dynasty may have been the gradual acceptance of Buddhism in China. ___
8) Like the Roman Empire, the Han Dynasty was weakened by its policy of permitting barbarians to settle within its borders. ___
9) Unlike the Roman Empire, however, it was a peasant revolt that ultimately overthrew the dynasty. ___
10) Belief in the virtues of the past and a pervasive moral order were hallmarks of the philosophy of Legalism. ___

MULTIPLE CHOICE: Select the response that best completes the sentence or answers the question.

1. "To correct the faults of the high, to rebuke the vices of the low, to suppress disorders, to decide against mistakes, to subdue the arrogant, to straighten the crooked, and to unify the folkways of the masses, ..."
   – This sums up the goals of the philosophy known as:
   a. Buddhism
   b. Confucianism
   c. Daoism
   d. Legalism

2. The "people of the Han" refers to all the people who:
   a. Lived within China's borders
   b. Were ethnically Chinese
   c. Accepted assimilation into Chinese culture
   d. Paid tribute to the Chinese emperors

3. Confucian-trained scholars and officials generally distrusted businessmen and merchants because:
   a. Merchants were on the lowest rung of the Confucian class system
   b. They were not believed to be loyal to the emperor
   c. They traded with the barbarians
   d. They were viewed as self-seeking and corrupt

4. Which of the following was not an accomplishment of the Fujiwara clan of Japan?
   a. The implementation of the "Taika Reforms"
   b. The adoption of the Chinese writing system and calendar
   c. The establishment of a new capital at Nara, modeled on Chang'an
   d. The building of many Buddhist temples, constructed on Chinese forms

5. Laozi (c. 604-517 B.C.E.) is regarded as the legendary founder of:
   a. Confucianism
   b. Daoism
   c. Legalism
   d. Shintoism

6. Which of the following was a significant Chinese invention of the period covered in the chapter?
   a. Gear mechanisms
   b. Woodblock printing
   c. The compass
   d. All of the above

7. Chinese territorial expansion under the Tang Dynasty differed from that under the Han Dynasty because the Tang:
    a. Tended to expand westward, while the Han expanded southward
    b. Occupied lands not inhabited by Chinese speakers
    c. Imperial acquisitions have remained under Chinese control ever since their conquest
    d. Successfully exported Buddhism into their conquered lands

8. Traditionally, _____ held many important positions within the imperial Chinese court.
    a. Buddhist monks
    b. Mongol slaves
    c. Eunuchs
    d. Royal concubines

9. The personal teachings of Confucius, as recorded by his disciples, are to be found in:
    a. *The Analects*
    b. *Admonitions of the Instructress of the Ladies in the Palace*
    c. The *Records of the Historian*
    d. The *I Ching* (*Book of Changes*)

10. Which of the following was <u>not</u> an important contribution of Qin Shi Huangdi and the Qin Dynasty?
    a. The standardization of the Chinese written language
    b. The completion of the Great Wall of China
    c. The establishment of Confucianism as the official government philosophy of China
    d. The establishment of the Chinese bureaucracy

11. The growth and acceptance of Buddhism in China was facilitated by its promotion by the _____ Dynasty.
    a. Qin
    b. Han
    c. Sui
    d. Tang

12. A dynasty's loss of its heavenly "Mandate" to rule China could be signaled by:
    a. Xiongnu invasions
    b. Flooding of the Huang He (Yellow River)
    c. Peasant revolts
    d. All of the above

13. Among the basic teachings of Confucianism were: respect for others, especially elders; reverence for tradition; the belief that the universe was governed by a moral order; the belief that character was more important to the making of a gentleman than birth; and –
    a. Reverence for nature
    b. The belief in the fundamental equality of all human beings
    c. Belief in strict laws and punishments
    d. Belief in the importance of human reason and education

14. The Grand Canal, linking the Huang Ho and Yangzi Rivers, Beijing and the seacoast, was completed under the:
    a. Qin Dynasty
    b. Han Dynasty
    c. Sui Dynasty
    d. Tang Dynasty

15. Which of the following neighbors of China and borrowers of Chinese culture was never under Chinese political control?
    a. Korea
    b. Japan
    c. Vietnam
    d. Turkestan

MAP ANALYSIS: The exercises on this page are based on the maps on pp. 213, 218, and 226.

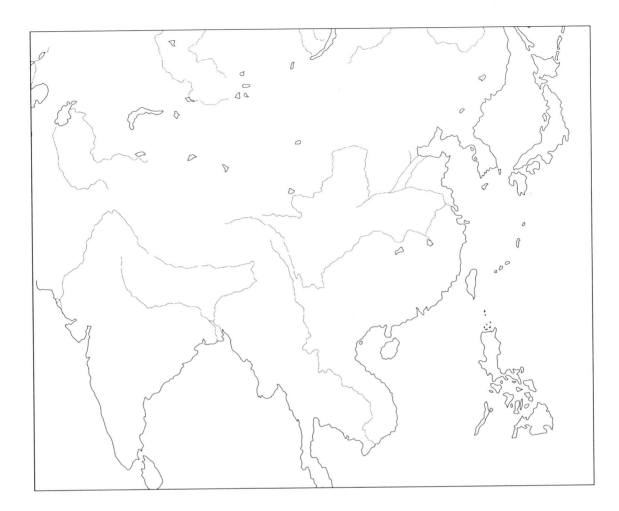

1. On the map above, locate and label each of the following:
   a. The boundaries of the Chinese Empire under the Qin, Han and Tang Dynasties
   b. Two of China's capital cities
   c. The site of a major Buddhist center during the Tang Dynasty
   d. The homeland of China's most troublesome "barbarian" neighbors
   e. Three neighboring countries which were heavily influenced by Chinese culture, but <u>not</u> absorbed by China
   f. China's two most important river systems
   g. China's two most extensive and important public construction works
   h. The route of the Silk Road
   i. China's most important port cities
   j. The general directional flow of Chinese population during the Han Dynasty

STUDY QUESTIONS: Consider each of the following questions carefully. Be prepared to supply specific evidence and examples to support your points in a class discussion or concise, well-organized, written essay.

1. Compare the reasons for the decline and fall of the Qin, Han and Tang Dynasties with the theoretical model for the reasons for the fall of empires at the beginning of Chapter 5. Which of the general causes for imperial decline can be applied in the case of each dynasty? (Cite specific examples.) How did Chinese historians and commentators explain the fall of their imperial dynasties? What factors or events might assume greater importance in their explanations?

2. What were the major contributions to the Chinese state and Chinese society of each of the four major dynasties discussed in this chapter; the Qin, Han, Sui and Tang? In what respects could each successive dynasty be said to have built upon the accomplishments of its predecessor?

3. Examine the nature and extent of Chinese influence on the development of one of the following neighboring societies: Korea, Vietnam, or Japan. What were some of the most important examples of Chinese influence in the country you have selected? <u>How and when</u> was Chinese influence exerted on the country?

HOW DO WE KNOW?

The following questions are based on the various illustrations or quotations and extracts from primary source documents and historical interpretations in the chapter.

1. The text asserts that Confucian influence remained strong in China throughout the period covered in this chapter. Examine this assertion with respect to the role and responsibilities of women in the Confucian world-view, demonstrating with specific examples the enduring influence of Confucian ideals and the status of women in the Confucian "Five Relationships."

2. Using the available sources in the chapter, compare the competing Chinese philosophies of Legalism and Confucianism. What are the most important values of each? How does each ideology view human beings? How does each seek to order and regulate society? What behaviors would be most highly prized in government officials by adherents of each belief system? Cite specific examples from the <u>primary source</u> documents.

3. "China exerted tremendous cultural evidence on her neighbors, but was herself also influenced by outside forces during the Han, Sui and Tang Dynasties." – Explain this statement, using evidence from illustrations in the text. What "forces" (peoples, religions, etc.) exerted an influence on China during this period, and how?

TRUE/FALSE ANSWERS: 1-T; 2-F; 3-T; 4-F; 5-F; 6-T; 7-T; 8-T; 9-T; 10-F

MULTIPLE CHOICE ANSWERS: 1-D; 2-C; 3-D; 4-B; 5-B; 6-D; 7-A; 8-C; 9-A; 10-C; 11-D; 12-D; 13-D; 14-C; 15-B

8 INDIAN EMPIRES

CULTURAL COHESION IN A DIVIDED SUBCONTINENT, 1500 B.C.E. – 1100 C.E.

KEY TOPICS
- New Arrivals in South Asia
- The Empires of India
- Invasions End the Age of Empires
- India, China, and Rome: Empires and Intermediate Institutions

CHAPTER NOTES

In the space provided below, construct your own outline of the chapter. Before you begin, refer to the "Key Topics" (section headings – above), introductory paragraph, chapter conclusion ("Indian Empires: What Difference Do They Make"?) and "Review Questions" to help you identify the major questions and issues covered in the chapter and the author's main arguments and interpretations. This will aid you in deciding what to include in your outline notes.

TRUE/FALSE QUESTIONS: Read each question carefully (answers at end of chapter).

1) Chandragupta Maurya, the founder of the Maurya Empire, published his laws on a series of rock and pillar edicts erected throughout India. ___
2) The Tamil people of southeastern India have preserved their own culture and language through centuries of rule by Aryan, Mughal and British conquerors. ___
3) Angkor Wat in modern day Cambodia and Borobudur on the island of Java (Indonesia) are examples of the cultural influence of "Greater India." ___
4) The *Artha-sastra* is an influential text of Mahayana Buddhism. ___
5) The dominant state languages of Maurya and Gupta India – Prakrit and Sanskrit – are related to the major European language groups, such as the Romance and Germanic languages. ___
6) Although seemingly intolerant and undemocratic, the caste system has served a useful cultural and social function throughout Indian history, by helping the subcontinent to absorb and assimilate new immigrants into Indian culture. ___
7) The early history of the Aryan migrations into India is most vividly illustrated by pottery and other archeological evidence. ___
8) The Gupta Empire was smaller in geographical extent than its Maurya predecessor, but exercised enormous cultural and religious influence on India. ___
9) The *Mahabharata,* the longest poem in world literature, traces the story of the mythical god-king Rama and his devoted wife Sita. ___
10) The teachings of Siddhartha Gautama were advanced in India by the conversion of the Emperor Asoka to his philosophy. ___

MULTIPLE CHOICE: Select the response which best completes the sentence or answers the question.

1. The Indo-Aryan language which became the main written language for Hindu religious texts and official government documents under the Gupta Dynasty was:
   a. *Brahmi*
   b. Prakrit
   c. Persian
   d. Sanskrit

2. India became an important trading partner with Rome, beginning with the reign of which of the following?
   a. Alexander the Great
   b. Asoka Maurya
   c. Augustus Caesar
   d. Attila the Hun

3. The Gandhara Buddha is thought to be a good example of _____ influence on Indian art.
   a. Chinese
   b. Hellenistic
   c. Roman
   d. Persian

4. The "justice of the fish" is a term referring to:
   a. Relationships among various Indian states
   b. The Hindu caste system
   c. India's relationship with southeast Asia
   d. All of the above

5. During the period between the Maurya and Gupta dynasties, much of northern India was unified under which of the following nomadic groups?
   a. Shakas
   b. Hunas
   c. Pallavas
   d. Kushanas

6. The Tamil peoples of southeast India are representative of:
    a. Nomadic invader groups in India
    b. Pre-Aryan native groups
    c. Survivors of the Maurya Dynasty
    d. Indo-Aryan speaking groups

7. Chandragupta Maurya may have first conceived of unifying all of India after contact with:
    a. Alexander the Great
    b. Asoka Maurya
    c. Augustus Caesar
    d. Attila the Hun

8. The Indian epic poem of the *Ramayana* is believed to describe:
    a. The "justice of the fishes"
    b. The rise of the Maurya Dynasty in Magadha
    c. The conquest of southern India by Indo-Aryan invaders
    d. A long civil war between two branches of the same Indo-Aryan family

9. Indian culture was spread throughout Southeast Asia by which of the following means?
    a. Buddhist missionaries
    b. Hindu merchants
    c. The expansion of the kingdom of Funan
    d. All of the above

10. Asoka Maurya is thought to have changed his philosophy of rule after converting to the teachings of:
    a. Kautilya
    b. Confucius
    c. Kalinga
    d. Buddha

11. Which of the following type of evidence for Roman trade with India is not mentioned in the text?
    a. Indian written sources
    b. Roman written sources
    c. Roman coins in India
    d. Evidence of Roman trading posts in India

12. The leadership of the *janapadas* was centered on:
    a. Religious cults
    b. Buddhist monks
    c. Family lineage groups
    d. Merchant alliances

13. Which of the following dynasties came closest to unifying the entire Indian subcontinent?
    a. Mauryas
    b. Guptas
    c. Kushanas
    d. Hunas

14. Which of the following was not a major result of the Hunas' invasions of India?
    a. The downfall of the Maurya Dynasty
    b. The weakening of the Gupta Empire
    c. The weakening of Buddhism in India
    d. The diversification of the Indian gene pool

15. Indian states tended to base their rule primarily upon:
    a. Military force
    b. Professional bureaucracies
    c. Merchant elites
    d. Traditional religious and social groups

MAP ANALYSIS

The maps on pp. 247, 252, 255, 274, and 284 should be used to complete the exercises below.

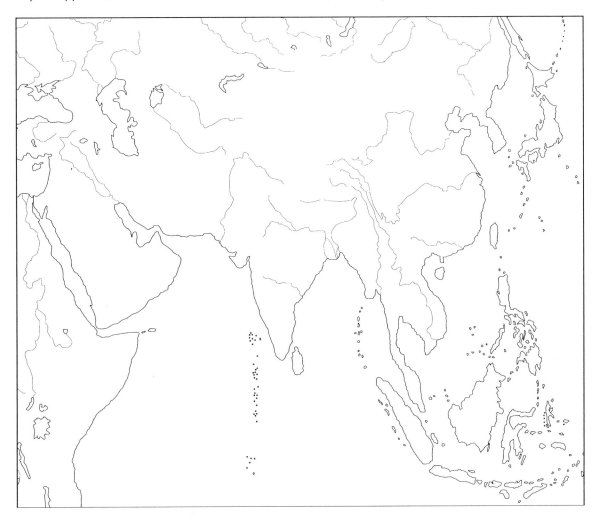

1. On the map above, locate and identify the following places and geographical features:
    a. The Indus and Ganges Rivers; the Himalaya and Hindu Kush Mountains; the Arabian Sea; and the Bay of Bengal
    b. Magadha; the Deccan; the Punjab; Simhala (Lanka); Gandhara; Gujarat
    c. Areas inhabited by the following peoples: Kushanas; Tamils; Cholas; Pallavas; Shakas
    d. Draw in the major trade routes emanating from India and the following places: Funan, Myanmar, Angkor, Borobudur.

2. Superimpose on the map the boundaries of the Maurya and Gupta Empires at their greatest extent. What regions of India escaped control by either empire. What may have been the causes for this? The results?

3. Encircle the areas referred to in the text as "Greater India." How does your map serve to illustrate how Indian cultural and religious influence was extended to these areas?

STUDY QUESTIONS: Consider each of the following questions carefully. Be prepared to supply specific evidence and examples to support your points in a class discussion or concise, well-organized written essay.

1. It could be argued that a combination of internal and external forces have been responsible for the fact that political unity within the Indian subcontinent has always been partial and short-lived. What are the principal reasons for this major aspect of Indian history?

2. Compare the major achievements and cultural legacies of early India's two most important imperial dynasties, the Mauryas and the Guptas. What were the most significant and lasting contributions of each to the development of Indian society and culture?

3. Contrast the ideas or governing put forth in the *Artha-sastra* with those promoted on Asoka's rock and pillar edicts. How do historians account for this change in attitude between the government of Chandragupta Maurya and his successor?

HOW DO WE KNOW?

1. How and when was Indian culture spread throughout southeast Asia? What evidence do we have for this cultural diffusion? Cite as many different examples and types of <u>primary source</u> evidence as you can in your answer.

2. In the absence of the sort of official histories that exist for China and the strong tradition of critical history writing such as existed in ancient Greece and Rome, what type of sources must historians of early India rely upon to construct their narratives and derive inferences? What can be learned from these sources? What biases might they exhibit? Cite specific examples from the <u>primary sources</u> to support your points.

3. India not only shares many common characteristics with the Greek-Macedonian, Roman and Chinese Empires but appears to have had extensive contacts with them. What sorts of contacts existed and what evidence survives to document these contacts? Again, cite as many pieces of <u>primary source</u> evidence as possible to support your answer.

TRUE/FALSE ANSWERS: 1-F; 2-T; 3-T; 4-F; 5-T; 6-T; 7-F; 8-T; 9-F; 10-T

MULTIPLE CHOICE ANSWERS: 1-D; 2-C; 3-B; 4-A; 5-D; 6-B; 7-A; 8-C; 9-D; 10-D; 11-A; 12-C; 13-A; 14-A; 15-D

9 HINDUISM AND BUDDHISM

THE SACRED SUBCONTINENT: THE SPREAD OF RELIGION IN INDIA AND BEYOND, 1500 B.C.E. – 1200 C.E.

KEY TOPICS
- Examining Religious Beliefs
- Hinduism
- Buddhism
- Comparing Hinduism and Buddhism

CHAPTER NOTES

In the space provided below, construct your own outline of the chapter. Before you begin, refer to the "Key Topics" (section headings – above), introductory paragraph, chapter conclusion ("Hinduism and Buddhism: What Difference Do They Make"?) and "Review Questions" to help you identify the major questions and issues covered in the chapter and the author's main arguments and interpretations. This will aid you in deciding what to include in your outline notes.

TRUE/FALSE QUESTIONS: Read each question carefully (answers at end of chapter).

1) The highest caste in the Hindu caste system are the *kshatriya,* warriors and nobles. ___
2) A feature common to all systems of religious belief is the creation of its own sacred calendar, marking dates for specific rituals, celebrations and fasts. ___
3) The religion of Jainism, begun by the teacher Mahavir (c. 540 B.C.E.), started as a Buddhist sect. ___
4) The "Noble Eightfold Path" prescribes a strict series of Buddhist religious rituals required to attain *Nirvana.* ___
5) Krishna, the eighth *avatar* (incarnation) of Vishnu, is one of the two central figures in the *Bhagavad-Gita,* an important segment of the Hindu epic, the *Mahabharata.* ___
6) The Hindu concept of *karma* refers to the set of religious and ethical duties to which every living creature in the universe is subject. ___
7) The introduction of the concepts of the *bodhisattvas* and the Maitreya Buddha, a suffering servant who would come to save humanity, are central elements of Mahayana Buddhism. ___
8) While Buddhism itself has been virtually extinct in India for almost a millennium, Jainism survives and flourishes as a minority faith in parts of India and is thought to have had an important influence on the Mahatma Gandhi in the 20th century. ___
9) A common element in both Hinduism and Buddhism is the "transience" of earthly life. ___
10) Modern scholars of religion believe that Hinduism was brought to India by Aryan invaders. ___

MULTIPLE CHOICE: Select the response that best completes the sentence or answers the question.

1. Which of the following is now believed to have been the most likely way that Hinduism and Buddhism were spread throughout southeast Asia?
   a. By military conquest
   b. By Hindu priests and Buddhist monks, invited by local rulers
   c. By merchants and traders, from India
   d. By the dissemination of printed texts, from China

2. Hinduism differs from other world religions in that:
   a. Many of its beliefs and practices derive from folk traditions.
   b. Its origins are not identified with a historical founder or specific event.
   c. Its followers pray to a number of different deities.
   d. All of the above.

3. Japanese call their native Shinto religion "the way of the *kami.*" Who or what are *kami*?
   a. Japanese emperors
   b. Shinto priests
   c. Religious scholars
   d. Spirits found in nature

4. The principal difference between the Hindu priesthood and the Buddhist *sangha* (monastic orders) was:
   a. Hindu priests exercised considerable political power at times.
   b. Buddhist monasteries sometimes became very wealthy.
   c. Buddhist monastic orders were open to all men regardless of caste.
   d. Hindu priests had no formal education.

5. The Hindu god Shiva is usually pictured dancing within a circle of fire, symbolizing:
   a. The *samsara,* or eternal cycle of creation and destruction
   b. The "Four Noble Truths"
   c. The four castes of Hindu society
   d. The preservation of good health and banishment of bad luck

6. Buddhism established itself in China and Japan through the efforts of:
   a. Chinese and Japanese rulers
   b. Pilgrims and missionaries
   c. Merchants and traders
   d. All of the above

7. The origins of the Indian caste system are explained and justified in which Hindu sacred text?
    a. The *Bhagavad-Gita*
    b. The *Ramayana*
    c. The *Rigveda*
    d. The *Brahmanas*

8. The Buddhist concept of *nirvana* is very similar, but not exactly the same as, the Hindu concept of:
    a. *samsara*
    b. *bodhisattva*
    c. *dharma*
    d. *moksha*

9. Theravada Buddhism is practiced today in which of the following sets of countries?
    a. Tibet, Burma (Myanmar), and China
    b. Japan, Korea, and Vietnam
    c. Sri Lanka, Thailand, and Burma (Myanmar)
    d. Vietnam, Tibet, and Cambodia

10. According to the "Four Noble Truths" all life is sorrow; and sorrow is:
    a. Caused by "thirst" (desire)
    b. An illusion (*maya*)
    c. The result of bad *karma*
    d. Ended by reincarnation (*samsara*)

11. Which of the following describes the caste system in India today?
    a. It has been legally outlawed by the government.
    b. It still plays an important role in Indian society and politics.
    c. It exists in the form of many small groups, rather than the four ancient castes.
    d. All of the above.

12. Which of the following was not a major reason for the decline of Buddhism in India?
    a. Muslim invasions of India
    b. The similarity of Mahayana Buddhism to Hinduism
    c. The fall of the Gupta Dynasty
    d. The attraction of *Bhakti* devotionalism

13. The important Hindu concepts of *atman, dharma, karma, samsara, maya, and moksha* are introduced in:
    a. The *Mahabharata*
    b. The *Rigveda*
    c. The *Bhagavad-Gita*
    d. The *Upanishads*

14. Which of the following was not an important side-effect of the spread of Buddhism to Japan?
    a. The creation of the *kana*, or phonetic Japanese syllabary
    b. The adoption of Buddhism as state religion by the Japanese emperors
    c. The introduction of a pure aesthetic dimension into Buddhist sacred art
    d. The furthering of national and cultural unity within Japan

15. Siddhartha Gautama's family is thought to have belonged to which Hindu caste?
    a. *brahmina* (priests)
    b. *kshatriya* (warriors)
    c. *vaishya* (merchants)
    d. *shudra* (laborers)

MAP ANALYSIS: Use the maps on pp. 274, 284, and 291 to complete the exercises on this page.

1. On the map above, locate and identify the following:
    a. The major land and sea trade routes of Asia. (Label the Silk Road.)
    b. Funan, Tibet, Korea, Champa, Ceylon (Sri Lanka), Srivijaya, Gujarat, Burma
    c. Kanya Kumari, Dunhuang, Pagan, Nara, Borobudur, Ellora, Ajanta, Sanchi
    d. Bay of Bengal, South China Sea, Malacca Straits, Irrawaddy River

2. Mark with an H the places listed in 1b and 1c that are associated with Hinduism. Mark those associated with Buddhism with a B.

3. Using the map on p. 274, discuss how Hinduism has served as a unifying force in Indian society throughout history and continues to do so even today. What general aspects of Hinduism – and organized religion in general – are illustrated by the map and many of the different places that appear on it?

STUDY QUESTIONS: Consider each of the following terms carefully. Be prepared to supply specific evidence and examples to support your points in a class discussion or concise, well-organized written essay.

1. Compare Hinduism and Buddhism, with respect to their major doctrines, their organization and their adaptability. How are they similar? What are their most significant differences?

2. Compare Theravada and Mahayana Buddhism. What are their most significant differences? Why did the split occur? What were its effects on the development of Buddhism?

3. Explain how and why Buddhism died out in India, yet was able to flourish throughout most of East Asia. How does the expansion of Buddhism throughout Asia illustrate the characteristics of a "world religion"?

HOW DO WE KNOW?

The following questions are based on the illustrations or quotations and extracts from primary source documents and historical interpretations in the chapter.

1. In the *Bhagavad-Gita*, the warrior Arjun is reluctant to go into battle against his blood relatives. What advice does he receive from the god Krishna about his dilemma? How does the Lord Krishna's advice illustrate the basic beliefs of Hinduism?

2. Using specific examples from the text, discuss how significant aspects of Hinduism and Buddhism can be illustrated and explained through the study of paintings, sculpture and architecture.

3. A major tenet of both Hinduism and Buddhism is that life on earth is *maya* (illusion) and transient (fleeting). Cite as many specific <u>primary sources</u> (documents or illustrations) as you can that might demonstrate this belief. Be sure to explain the relevance of your sources.

TRUE/FALSE ANSWERS: 1-F; 2-T; 3-F; 4-F; 5-T; 6-F; 7-T; 8-T; 9-T; 10-F

MULTIPLE CHOICE ANSWERS: 1-B; 2-B; 3-D; 4-C; 5-A; 6-D; 7-C; 8-D; 9-C; 10-A; 11-D; 12-D; 13-D; 14-B; 15-B

10   JUDAISM AND CHRISTIANITY

PEOPLES OF THE BIBLE: GOD'S EVOLUTION IN WEST ASIA AND EUROPE, 1700 B.C.E. – 1100 C.E.

KEY TOPICS
- **Judaism**
- **Christianity**
- **Christianity in the Wake of Empire**

CHAPTER NOTES

In the space provided below, construct your own outline of the chapter. Before you begin, refer to the "Key Topics" (section headings – above), introductory paragraph, chapter conclusion ("Early Christianity: What Difference Does It Make"?) and "Review Questions" to help you identify the major questions and issues covered in the chapter and the author's main arguments and interpretations. This will aid you in deciding what to include in your outline notes.

TRUE/FALSE QUESTIONS: Read each question carefully (answers at end of chapter).

1) The term TaNaKh refers to the first five books of the Old Testament or Hebrew Bible. ___
2) Of the four major Jewish religious factions in Roman Judaea, the teachings of Jesus Christ were most similar to those of the Zealots. ___
3) Belief in divine salvation and an afterlife in heaven is not one of the essential beliefs of Judaism found in early Hebrew scripture. ___
4) There are no important female figures in the early Hebrew scriptures. ___
5) The Dead Sea Scrolls comprise the oldest surviving texts of the Old Testament, dating from the 2nd century B.C.E. ___
6) Under the influence of St. Augustine, early Christianity was heavily influenced by the ideas of the pagan Greek philosopher Plato. ___
7) A primary motive of Pope Gregory I in supporting the establishment of Christian monasteries was the role he thought they could play in the conversion of barbarians to Christianity. ___
8) The concept of "Original Sin," a crucial Christian teaching, was formulated by the apostle Paul. ___
9) Christianity was declared the only legal religion of the Roman Empire by the Emperor Constantine. __
10) Many Christian holidays and festivals, including Easter and Pentecost, correspond to important events on the Jewish sacred calendar. ___

MULTIPLE CHOICE: Select the response that completes the sentence or answers the question best.

1. Which of the following Jewish teachings is not included in the *Torah*?
    a. The covenant between God and his Chosen people
    b. The Ten Commandments
    c. The prophets' demands for just rulers
    d. A "Promised Land" in Israel

2. Jesus' preaching, though universalist in its message, seems to have been especially attractive to:
    a. The Zealots
    b. Roman soldiers
    c. The poor
    d. The Pharisees

3. The first Frankish king to convert to Christianity was which of the following?
    a. Clovis
    b. Charles Martel
    c. Pepin
    d. Charlemagne

4. The term "diaspora" is used to refer to Jews who were forcibly removed from Israel by:
    a. Assyrians
    b. Babylonians
    c. Romans
    d. All of the above

5. Biblical scholars attribute the compilation of the *Torah* (the first five books of the *Old Testament*) to:
    a. King Josiah
    b. King Solomon
    c. The prophet Isaiah
    d. Moses

6. The followers of Bishop Arius were condemned as heretics at the Council of Nicaea because:
    a. They accepted the authority of the Patriarch of Constantinople over that of the Roman Pope
    b. They refused to accept Paul's doctrine of salvation by faith alone
    c. They refused to accept the divinity of Jesus and his indivisibility from God
    d. They refused to abandon the Jewish sabbath and dietary laws

7. St. Augustine's introduction of Neoplatonic elements into Christian theology is thought to have facilitated the religion's intellectual acceptance in the Roman Empire and reinforced:
    a. The attraction of meditation and monasticism
    b. The attraction of Christianity among barbarian tribes
    c. The separation of church and state
    d. All of the above

8. Which of the following best describes the relationship between the teachings of Jesus and his apostles and the core doctrines of Judaism?
    a. They accepted the teachings contained in the TaNaKh, but rejected the authority of Jewish leaders.
    b. They accepted the moral message of Judaism, but rejected Jewish legalism and separatism.
    c. They added the concept of "Love your neighbor" to the Jewish commandment to love God.
    d. All of the above.

9. Some scholars have speculated that the concept of monotheism may have been promoted in Judaism:
    a. During the Jewish captivity in Egypt
    b. As a result of the destruction of Israel by Sennacherib of Assyria
    c. By the preaching of the prophets
    d. During the Jewish captivity in Babylonia

10. Which of the following ideas or beliefs is not to be found in the Gnostic Gospels?
    a. The suggestion that Jesus may have had a physical relationship with Mary Magdalene
    b. A questioning of the assumption that Jesus was the Son of God
    c. A greater role for women in the search for religious truth
    d. The idea that each individual could find God within himself or herself, without belief in Jesus

11. The primary cause of the Great Schism of 1054 between the Roman Catholic and orthodox branches of Christianity was:
    a. The Iconoclast Controversy
    b. The refusal of the Orthodox Church to use Latin in its services
    c. The refusal of the Orthodox Church to accept the results of the Council of Nicaea
    d. The refusal of the Orthodox Church to accept the authority of the Roman Pope

12. Which of the following seems to have been an important reason for the popularity of Christianity in the Roman Empire?
    a. Stories of Jesus' miracles
    b. The promise of salvation, irrespective of wealth, nationality or gender
    c. The austere and exemplary morals of the early Christians
    d. All of the above

13. The story of Esther in the Old Testament relates an episode of Jewish history during:
    a. The Babylonian Captivity
    b. The Exodus from Egypt
    c. The Jewish diaspora in the Persian Empire
    d. The era of the Jewish prophets

14. The Jewish prophets preached in reaction against:
    a. Divisions in Judaism among Pharisees, Sadducees, Zealots, and Essenes
    b. The immorality of Jewish society and the injustices of its rulers
    c. The conquest of Israel by the Romans
    d. The growth of Christianity within a Jewish society

15. The relative position of women in Jewish and Christian theology is best described in which of the following sentences?
    a. Women occupied a higher position in Christian teachings than in traditional Jewish teachings.
    b. Women occupied a higher position in traditional Jewish teachings than they did in Christian teachings.
    c. Women occupied a subordinate position to men in the teachings of both Judaism and Christianity.
    d. Christianity followed Judaism in according women equality with men.

MAP ANALYSIS

A. The following exercise is based on the maps on pp. 310 and 322

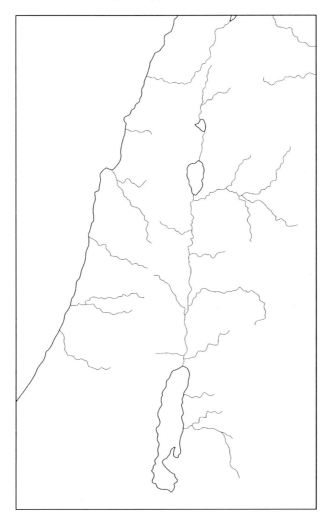

1. On the map above, locate and label the following:
    a. The boundaries of the kingdom of Israel under David and Solomon; and the boundaries of the later kingdoms of Israel and Judaea after 930 B.C.E.
    b. The Mediterranean Sea; Red Sea; Dead Sea and Sea of Galilee
    c. Sinai; Jerusalem; Damascus; Bethlehem; Nazareth; Tyre and Jericho (Underline the names of those places associated with Jesus.)
    d. The boundaries of the areas under Roman administration and under King Herod at the time of Jesus

2. Discuss how the divisions illustrated on the map ("The Kingdom of Israel") on p. 310 contributed to the conquest of Israel by the Assyrians and Babylonians and the subsequent diaspora of the Hebrew people. In what ways did these events influence the development of Judaism?

3. Discuss how the divisions illustrated on the map ("Palestine at the Time of Jesus") on p. 322 may have contributed to the development of factions within Judaism and the origins of Christianity. What specific places are associated with some of those factions?

B. The following exercise is based on the maps on pp. 154, 168, 320, and 326.

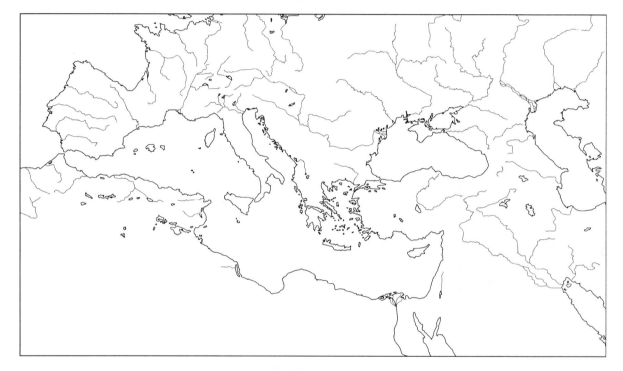

1. On the map above, locate and label each of the following:
    a. Areas settled by Jews during the diaspora
    b. The routes of the missionary journeys of Paul
    c. The approximate boundaries of Alexander's conquests and the Roman and Byzantine empires
    d. The regions which eventually followed Roman Catholic and Eastern Orthodox Christianity, respectively
    e. The cities of Jerusalem; Rome; Constantinople; Alexandria; Antioch; Athens and Tarsus
    f. Charlemagne's kingdom

2. Viewing the completed map above, consider the possible relationships between Judaism, the Hellenistic Ecumene, the Roman Empire and the Christian religion. In what respects were St. Paul and St. Augustine symbolic of those relationships?

STUDY QUESTIONS: Consider each of the following questions carefully. Be prepared to supply specific evidence and examples to support your points in a class discussion or concise, well-organized written essay.

1. Explain the attraction of Christianity to many in the Roman Empire, even during times of official persecution. Among which groups was it apparently most popular? Why is this thought to be the case?

2. According to the text, "The Jewish belief in one god, monotheism, was not simply a reduction in the number of gods from many to one." – What does Spodek mean by that statement? What, in addition to having only one god, does "monotheism" imply?

3. Discuss the roles of monasticism, missionaries, and rulers in the expansion of Christianity, citing specific examples in your explanation. How do their respective roles compare with their counterparts in Asia, regarding the spread of Hinduism and Buddhism?

HOW DO WE KNOW?

The following questions are based on the various illustrations or quotations and extracts from primary source documents and historical interpretations in the chapter.

1. Trace the "evolution of the image of God" – or the perceptions of Jewish and Christian writers regarding the nature and powers of God, as revealed in the primary source extracts and quotations in Chapter 10, from the *Torah* to St. Augustine's *City of God.*

2. According to the text, what were the major contributions of the great Jewish Prophets (Isaiah, Amos, Jeremiah and Micah) to Judaism? Support your answer with specific examples.

3. The text states that Jesus "sounded much like a latter day Jewish prophet calling his people to reform," in his "Sermon on the Mount." What does the author mean by this statement? How do Jesus' words – and perhaps the general tone of his preaching, resemble those of the earlier prophets and place him within the Jewish tradition?

TRUE/FALSE ANSWERS: 1-F; 2-F; 3-T; 4-F; 5-T; 6-T; 7-T; 8-T; 9-F; 10-T

MULTIPLE CHOICE ANSWERS: 1-C; 2-C; 3-A; 4-D; 5-A; 6-C; 7-A; 8-B; 9-A; 10-B; 11-D; 12-D; 13-C; 14-B; 15-C

11   ISLAM

SUBMISSION TO ALLAH: MUSLIM CIVILIZATION
BRIDGES THE WORLD, 570 C.E. – 1500 C.E.

KEY TOPICS
- **The Origins of Islam**
- **Successors to the Prophet**
- **Spiritual, Religious, and Cultural Flowering**
- **Relations with Non-Muslims**

CHAPTER NOTES

In the space provided below, construct your own outline of the chapter. Before you begin, refer to the "Key Topics" (section headings – above), introductory paragraph, chapter conclusion ("Judaism, Christianity, and Islam: What Difference Do They Make"?) and "Review Questions" to help you identify the major questions and issues covered in the chapter and the author's main arguments and interpretations. This will aid you in deciding what to include in your outline notes.

TRUE/FALSE QUESTIONS: Read each question carefully (answers at end of chapter).

1) The Sunni-Shi'ite split in Islam occurred over a dispute concerning the legitimate successor to Muhammad and not because of any particular differences in religious doctrine. ___
2) The Abbasid Caliphate was established by Seljuk Turks in 750 C.E., with its capital at Baghdad. ___
3) Contrary to common belief among non-Muslims, Islam received more voluntary converts in its early days than forced conversions through Arab military conquests. ___
4) Today, a single code of Islamic law (the *shari'a*) unites Muslims in all parts of the *dar al-Islam*. ___
5) Muslim scholars disagree over the exact meaning of *jihad:* while some interpret it to mean a holy war in defense of Islam, others understand it as a personal call to the individual to lead a spiritual life. ___
6) According to the *Quran*, Muhammad was neither divine, nor even the founder of a new doctrine, but only a messenger of God's truth. ___
7) The *shari'a* – Islamic law – is interpreted by trained officials known as Sufis. ___
8) *Dhimmi* status – that of a tolerated and protected religious minority – was extended by Muslim rulers only to so-called "Peoples of the Book," or adherents of monotheistic religions. ___
9) Like Judaism and Christianity, Islam embraces believers in both mystical and rationalist practices. ___
10) By 1600, Islam had established itself as far away from its Arabian birthplace as the Philippine Islands and West Africa. ___

MULTIPLE CHOICE: Select the response that completes the sentence or answers the question best.

1. "Twelver" Shi'as look forward to the reappearance of the twelfth or "Hidden" *imam* (religious leader), whom they call the _____, or Muslim messiah.
    a. *mahdi*
    b. *Aga Khan*
    c. *sufi*
    d. *qadi*

2. Muhammad is viewed and described in the Muslim religion as the:
    a. "Son of Allah"
    b. Founder of Islam and the first Muslim
    c. "Messenger of God"
    d. All of the above

3. Which of the following examples of Islamic architecture was built as a mausoleum (tomb for the dead)?
    a. The Alhambra in Granada, Spain
    b. The Dome of the Rock in Jerusalem
    c. The Mihrab in Cordoba, Spain
    d. The Taj Mahal in Agra, India

4. Which of the following most accurately describes the expansion of the first (Ummayad) Islamic empire?
    a. Arab military conquest, accompanied by forced conversions to Islam
    b. Arab military conquest, followed by forced assimilation
    c. Arab military conquest, followed by voluntary conversions to Islam
    d. Arab military conquest, which discouraged assimilation and conversions to Islam

5. The Abbasid Caliphate officially ruled most of the core Islamic world from 749 to 1258, when the last caliph was overthrown and executed by the Mongols, but in actuality Abbasid rule had been steadily weakened after c. 900, due to:
    a. Slave revolts and military mutinies
    b. The establishment of quasi-independent states in Egypt and north Africa
    c. Invasions by the Seljuk Turks
    d. All of the above

6. Al-Gazzali (1058-1111) is revered as "The Renewer of Islam" owing to his writings, which:
    a. Achieved a reconciliation between the *Sunni* and *Shi'a* branches of the religion
    b. Achieved a reconciliation between mystical Sufism and rationality within Islam
    c. Enabled Persian to become the second language of Islam, along with Arabic
    d. Abandoned his earlier support of the Mutazalites and embraced traditional religious belief

7. Which of the following other world religions was never granted *dhimmi* status under Islamic domination?
    a. Buddhism
    b. Christianity
    c. Hinduism
    d. Judaism

8. Ibn Sina (known as Avicenna in Europe), in addition to being a noted rationalist Islamic philosopher, also played an important role in disseminating knowledge of the science of _____ throughout the Islamic and Christian world.
    a. Algebra
    b. Agriculture
    c. Medicine
    d. Alchemy

9. Religious and legal principles of Islam were taught in special academies, or centers of learning, known as:
    a. *Ulamas*
    b. *Ummas*
    c. *Shari'as*
    d. *Madrasas*

10. In the 10th Century, Abd al-Rahman established a Muslim caliphate independent of the Abbasids in:
    a. Spain
    b. India
    c. Egypt
    d. Persia

11. Which of the following descriptions is most accurate in describing Islam as a world religion and a civilization?
    a. Uniformity in religion and law, with wide regional social and cultural variations
    b. Uniformity in law, language (Arabic) and culture, with variation in religious beliefs
    c. A community of shared religious beliefs, law, and culture, with significant regional variations
    d. A completely uniform religious, legal and cultural community

12. Sufis have played an important role in the development of Islam, as:
    a. Teachers in Islamic academies
    b. Men and women who emphasized the devotional aspects of prayer, fasting and music
    c. Judges and interpreters of Islamic law
    d. Slave soldiers who spread Islam in Arab and Turkish armies

13. Which of the following is not regarded as one of the "Five Pillars" of Islam?
    a. *Ramadan*
    b. *Hajj*
    c. *Jihad*
    d. Alms

14. Which of the following was disseminated throughout the Islamic world by scholars and technicians?
    a. Chinese paper-making techniques
    b. Greek and Persian medical knowledge
    c. Indian mathematical concepts
    d. All of the above

15. A rationalist movement within Islam, which argued against a literal interpretation of the *Quran*, was called the _____, meaning "those who keep themselves apart."
    a. Ghaznavids
    b. *Qadis*
    c. Mutazilites
    d. Almohads

MAP ANALYSIS: The following exercise is based on the maps on pp. 354, 360, and 361.

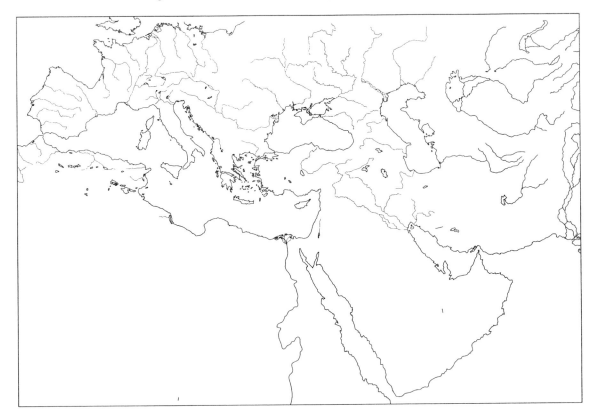

1. On the map above, locate and label the following:
   a. Muhammad's birthplace <u>and</u> the city to which he fled to escape persecution
   b. The capitals of the Ummayad <u>and</u> Abbasid Caliphates
   c. An important center of Muslim learning in west Africa
   d. The primary objective of the First Crusade
   e. The site of the Alhambra
   f. Areas ruled by the Almoravids <u>and</u> Almohads

2. Indicate with directional arrows the following military invasions and conquests:
   a. The expansion of the Ummayad Caliphate
   b. The invasions of the Seljuk Turks (Label the site of their victory over the Byzantine Empire in 1071.)
   c. The Crusades
   d. The Mongol invasions (Label the site of their defeat by Arab armies in 1260.)
   e. The *Reconquista*

B. The following exercise is based on the maps on pp. 360, 361, 362, 363, and 364.

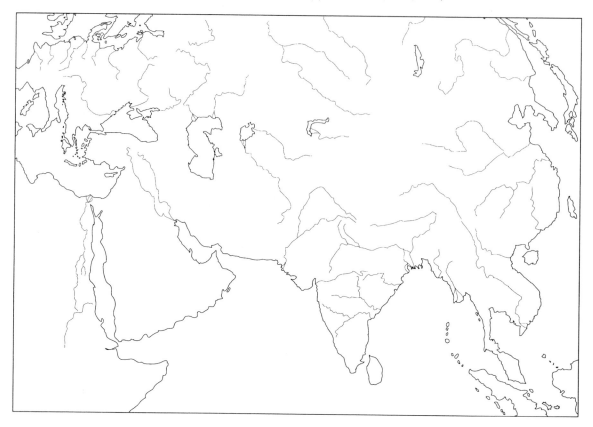

1. On the map above, shade in and label the following:
   a. The boundaries of the Ghaznavid Empire
   b. The boundaries of the Delhi Sultanate
   c. The region of Bengal
   d. The boundaries of the Empire of Timur
   e. The extent of Muslim expansion in Southeast Asia, by 1600

2. Which of the shaded areas above came under Muslim influence primarily by military conquest? Which ones were converted to Islam by other means? Describe those different means.

STUDY QUESTIONS: Consider each of the following questions carefully. Be prepared to supply specific evidence and examples to support your points in a class discussion or concise, well-organized written essay.

1. Explain the historical origins of the schism between *Sunni* and *Shi'a* Islam. In what respects do the actual religious beliefs and practices of Sunnis and Shi'ites differ? In what countries or regions does each group predominate today?

2. The centralized Muslim empire of the Umayyad and Abbasid Caliphates effectively lasted for only a few centuries, yet Islam as a religious and cultural force continued to expand and flourish. The text discusses a number of reasons for this. Discuss at least two of these factors in detail, citing specific examples from the chapter.

3. Discuss the treatment of non-Muslim peoples under Muslim rule. What was the attitude of Muslim conquerors and rulers toward their various non-Muslim subjects?

HOW DO WE KNOW?

The following questions are based on the various illustrations or quotations and extracts from primary source documents and historical interpretations in the chapter.

1. List and explain the "Five Pillars of Islam." How were they originally communicated to the Muslim faithful? What teachings or principles are considered to be among the core beliefs of Islam?

2. Spodek argues that, contrary to popular belief, forced conversion to Islam by Arab, Turkish or Persian military conquerors was the exception, rather than the rule. That being the case, how do scholars account for the massive conversions to Islam which took place, especially in areas outside the Muslim heartland, such as North Africa, Spain, India, and central and southeast Asia? What factors were important in motivating conversion?

3. One of the most controversial historical questions regarding Islam concerns its effects on the status of women and on gender relations in the areas that came under its influence. Explain the several positions historians have taken on this issue. What inferences or generalizations could you make, based on the sources in this chapter?

TRUE/FALSE ANSWERS: 1-T; 2-F; 3-T; 4-F; 5-T; 6-T; 7-F; 8-F; 9-T; 10-T

MULTIPLE CHOICE ANSWERS: 1-A; 2-C; 3-D; 4-C; 5-D; 6-B; 7-A; 8-C; 9-D; 10-A; 11-C; 12-B; 13-C; 14-D; 15-C

12   ESTABLISHING WORLD TRADE ROUTES

THE GEOGRAPHY AND PHILOSOPHIES OF
EARLY ECONOMIC SYSTEMS –
TRADE AND TRADERS: GOALS AND FUNCTIONS, 1000 – 1500

KEY TOPICS:
- **World Trade: An Historical Analysis**
- **Trade Networks**
- **Trade in the Americas before 1500**
- **Trade in Sub-Saharan Africa**
- **Muslim and Jewish Traders**
- **Asia's Complex Trade Patterns**
- **The Mongols**

CHAPTER NOTES

In the space provided below, construct your own outline of the chapter. Before you begin, refer to the "Key Topics" (section headings – above), introductory paragraph, chapter conclusion ("Legacies to the Present: What Difference Do They Make"?) and "Review Questions" to help you identify the major questions and issues covered in the chapter and the author's main arguments and interpretations. This will aid you in deciding what to include in your outline notes.

TRUE/FALSE QUESTIONS: Read each question carefully (answers at end of chapter).

1) *"Pax Mongolica"* is a term referring to the spread of bubonic plague along Mongol trade routes. ___
2) Arab merchants sailed the Indian Ocean in ships built of teak planks stitched together with coconut fibers and rigged with lateen sails. ___
3) The fundamental difference between local and international trade in the period covered in this chapter was that local trade dealt in the necessities of life, while international trade dealt in luxury goods. ___
4) The peoples of Mesoamerica and South America carried on an extensive interregional trade. ___
5) Indian Ocean trade was conducted mainly from different emporia, from which goods were trans-shipped, rather than being carried in one ship for their entire voyage. ___
6) While much of the Indian Ocean trade was dominated by Arab merchants, Chinese coins and paper money were the most popular currency. ___
7) Considerable evidences exists that Marco Polo, author of the most famous European account of China under Mongol rule, may never have visited the places he described. ___
8) Polynesian sailors were among the most accomplished traders along the Indian Ocean routes. ___
9) Tales of Mongol brutality and terror may reflect their authors' bias, since there are virtually no native Mongol accounts of their people's history or conquests. ___
10) The Arab world's counterpart to Marco Polo's travels were those of the 14th century traveler Sinbad, whose accounts of India, China and Southeast Asia are a valuable source for those areas. ___

MULTIPLE CHOICE: Select the response that completes the sentence or answers the question best.

1. East Africa was brought into the Eurasian trading system in the 9th century by the:
   a. Arrival of Arab merchants via the Indian Ocean
   b. Introduction of the camel
   c. Voyages of Admiral Zheng He
   d. Arrival of Portuguese explorers

2. In a completely "free market economy," prices would vary only according to the:
   a. Location of the market
   b. Needs of the poor
   c. Relationship between the supply of goods and the demand for them
   d. Effort of the merchant

3. In the Inca Empire, the economic specialties of different regions were determined mainly by:
   a. Their proximity to the Pacific Ocean
   b. The state and its semi-divine rulers
   c. The demands of Spanish traders
   d. Their relative altitude in the Andes Mountains

4. The short-lived existence of the vast Mongol Empire can be attributed mainly to:
   a. The Mongol tendency to intermarry with local peoples and convert to local religions
   b. Succession disputes within the family of Chinggis Khan
   c. Inability to adapt to conditions of settled life and administration
   d. All of the above

5. In earlier times, luxury goods comprised the major portion of long-distance trade because:
   a. Of their value relative to their weight
   b. They were in heavy demand
   c. They were bartered in exchange for other goods
   d. Their transportation costs were subsidized by regional rulers

6. Under the Mongol and Ming dynasties in China, the principal producers of cotton cloth were:
   a. Urban guild members
   b. Government-owned slaves
   c. Rural peasant women
   d. Jewish merchants

7. In the Aztec Empire, long-distance trade was controlled by merchant guilds called:
    a. *Pochteca*
    b. *Quipu*
    c. *Lateens*
    d. *Jongs*

8. The most likely purpose of the seven voyages of the Chinese admiral Zheng He was to:
    a. Establish new trade routes free from Mongol control
    b. Collect tribute from rulers and trading cities along the routes of the expeditions
    c. Extend the political control of the Ming Emperor
    d. Seek new markets for Chinese goods

9. The best examples of governments which derived their power and wealth by controlling traders and trade routes, rather than land and agriculture, during the period covered in the chapter, were the:
    a. Aztec and Inca empires of the Americas
    b. Ming Dynasty China
    c. Mongol Khanates
    d. West African kingdoms of Ghana, Mali and Songhay

10. Which of the following areas was never successfully conquered by the Mongols?
    a. China
    b. Japan
    c. Iraq
    d. Russia

11. An unintended consequence of the *Pax Mongolica*, or "Mongol Peace" may have been the:
    a. Introduction of the camel into North Africa
    b. Introduction of feudalism into Europe
    c. Introduction of the bubonic plague into Europe
    d. All of the above

12. Sub-Saharan Africa's earliest indigenous empires developed in the Niger River Valley, in the geographical region known as:
    a. The Swahili coast
    b. Great Zimbabwe
    c. The Congo
    d. The Sahel

13. Large networks of long-distance merchants who encouraged and conducted trade throughout the world with their home societies are known as:
    a. *Pochteca*
    b. Trade diasporas
    c. Guilds
    d. Emporia

14. Which of the following was a possible reason for the Ming Dynasty's halting of the voyages of Zheng He?
    a. The reconstruction of the Grand Canal and a renewed emphasis on domestic trade
    b. Renewed emphasis on the defense of China's northern borders vs. the Mongols
    c. The desire to reduce piracy and smuggling
    d. All of the above

15. The wealth of the Muslim Empire of Mali is best demonstrated by its greatest ruler:
    a. Mansa Musa
    b. Ibn Battuta
    c. Sinbad
    d. Hülegü

MAP ANALYSIS: The following exercise is based on the maps on pp. 398, 405, 406, 418, and 420.

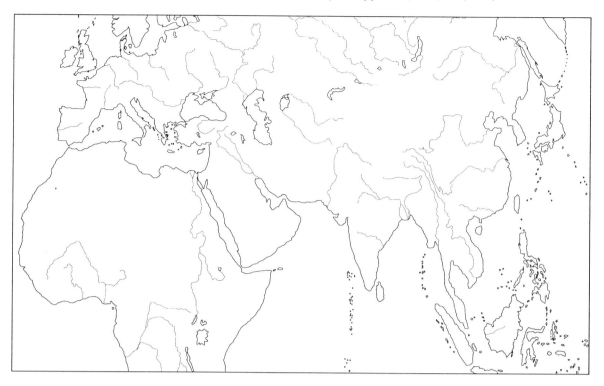

1. On the map above locate and mark the following:
    a. The major trading ports and of: Hangzhou, Canton, Malacca, Macassar, Calicut, Cambay, Muscat, Hormuz, Aden, Zanzibar, and Kilwa
    b. The cities of Fez, Timbuktu, Jenne, Sofala, and Great Zimbabwe
    c. The Sahara Desert, Himalaya Mountains, Indian Ocean, and South China Sea

2. Trace or outline each of the following:
    a. The African trading kingdoms/empires of Ghana, Mali and Songhay
    b. The travel routes of Ibn Batutta and Marco Polo
    c. The four Mongol successor kingdoms of the empire of Chinggis Khan
    d. The routes of the spread of bubonic plague in the 14th century

STUDY QUESTIONS: Consider each of the following questions carefully. Be prepared to supply specific evidence and examples to support your points in a class discussion or a concise, well-organized written essay.

1. According to the author of the text, "Societies … regulate trade to some degree in order to serve the greater good of the society. … Business may be more regulated or less regulated, but it is never completely unregulated." (pp. 392-393) Cite at least three examples of such regulation from the chapter. In each case, who was actually regulating trade and how? How was the "greater good" being protected?

2. From approximately 750 to 1500 C.E., central Asian, trans-Saharan and Indian Ocean trade routes were dominated by Muslim traders, mostly Arabs, Berbers and Persians. What are the most likely reasons for this Muslim dominance? What were some of its principal effects? Cite specific examples from the text.

3. Between 1407 and 1433, the Ming Emperor of China sent his great Admiral Zheng He on seven great seaborne expeditions, extending as far as India, the Persian Gulf and east Africa. But the voyages were discontinued and never followed up by the extension of Chinese political or commercial control to those areas, in spite of the fact that China was probably the richest and most powerful country in the world. Why was this the case? And what, according to many historians, were some of the consequences of this withdrawal?

HOW DO WE KNOW?

The following questions are based on the various illustrations or quotations and extracts from primary source documents and historical interpretations in the chapter.

1. What inferences and generalizations about long-distance trade can you make on the basis of the fragmentary excerpts from the *Rihla* of the Muslim traveler Ibn Battuta and the *Travels of Marco Polo*? How might they support some of the major points made in the chapter?

2. Based on the extracts from *The Travels of Marco Polo* (p. 413), the accounts of Ibn Battuta (p. 410) and Pao Hui (p. 413); the scroll painting by Zhang Deduan (p. 412) and the poem Xu Xianzhong (p. 413), who were the "winners" and "losers" in the Chinese economy of the time? What social groups or individuals prospered? Who were exploited?

3. Based on the evidence discussed in this chapter, was the overall impact of the Mongols on the history of Asia and the world a positive or negative one? What evidence and examples should be emphasized? What are some possible problems involved in the making of such an historical assessment?

TRUE/FALSE ANSWERS: 1-F; 2-T; 3-T; 4-F; 5-T; 6-T; 7-T; 8-F; 9-T; 10-F

MULTIPLE CHOICE ANSWERS: 1-A; 2-C; 3-B; 4-D; 5-A; 6-C; 7-A; 8-B; 9-D; 10-B; 11-C; 12-D; 13-B; 14-D; 15-A

13   EUROPEAN VISIONS

ECONOMIC GROWTH, RELIGION AND RENAISSANCE, GLOBAL CONNECTIONS, 1100 – 1776

KEY TOPICS
- The Atlantic
- The Decline of Trade in the Mediterranean
- Trade and Social Change in Europe
- The Renaissance
- A New World
- Oceania

CHAPTER NOTES

In the space provided below, construct your own outline of the chapter. Before you begin, refer to the "Key Topics" (section headings – above), introductory paragraph, chapter conclusion ("Legacies to the Future: What Difference Do They Make"?) and "Review Questions" to help you identify the major questions and issues covered in the chapter and the author's main arguments and interpretations. This will aid you in deciding what to include in your outline notes.

TRUE/FALSE QUESTIONS: Read each question carefully (answers at end of chapter).

1) By the year 950, control of the Mediterranean Sea was divided among three groups, the Muslims to the south and southeast, the Byzantine Empire in the northeast, and the Vikings in the West. ___
2) The Kingdom of Portugal was ideally suited to become a leader in world exploration because of its great wealth and economic power. ___
3) The Renaissance humanist Petrarch devoted his life to the study of Muslim commentaries on Aristotle. ___
4) The growth or urban economies in Europe provided the opportunity for some upward economic mobility among workers, but also increased social and economic tensions in the cities. ___
5) A major advantage of Portuguese ships in the Indian Ocean was their deployment of cannon. ___
6) Renaissance humanism was essentially a secular and materialistic development, without any religious influence. ___
7) The English explorer Captain James Cook was the first European navigator to survey the coast of Australia. ___
8) St. Thomas Aquinas argued that Aristotelian logic and Christian theology were not in conflict. ___
9) Industrial and commercial activity in medieval European cities flourished because it was essentially unregulated by their governments or any other agencies. ___
10) Competition for profits among different groups of European traders was a more important obstacle to Mediterranean trade than warfare between Christian and Muslim states in the Middle Ages. ___

MULTIPLE CHOICE: Select the response that completes the sentence or answers the question best.

1. Which of the following developments was <u>not</u> a result or side-effect of economic recovery in medieval Europe?
   a. Modification of Christian attitudes towards trade and profit
   b. A rise in class tensions between *bourgeois* employers and their employees
   c. Greater tolerance towards Jews
   d. The granting of town charters by regional rulers

2. The principal motivation of Portugal's Prince Henry the Navigator in fostering overseas exploration was:
   a. To spread Christianity in the New World
   b. To find a trade route to Asia free from control by the Ottoman Turks
   c. To prove that the earth was round
   d. All of the above

3. Which of the following European technological advance of the period 1100-1500 was <u>not</u> originally a European invention?
   a. Gunpowder weapons
   b. The decimal system
   c. Printing with movable type
   d. All of the above

4. The most noteworthy cultural and intellectual achievements of the Italian Renaissance occurred in Florence, under the patronage of:
   a. Avicenna
   b. The Medici family
   c. Italian Humanists
   d. Leonardo da Vinci

5. Chapter 12 ("Establishing World Trade Routes") focuses heavily on the Indian Ocean as an economic and cultural unit. This approach was pioneered by historian Fernand Braudel, who studied the:
   a. Pacific Ocean
   b. North Sea
   c. Mediterranean Sea
   d. Atlantic Ocean

6. The Portuguese explorer Vasco da Gama sailed around the coast of Africa and reached India in 1498, thus completing the route pioneered by:
    a. Bartolomeu Dias
    b. Christopher Columbus
    c. Ferdinand Magellan
    d. Amerigo Vespucci

7. Which of the following development was <u>not</u> an important precursor of the Renaissance of the 15th Century?
    a. The influence of Muslim philosophers
    b. A rise in urban economic activity in Europe
    c. The opening of European trade routes with India
    d. The writings of St. Thomas Aquinas

8. The leading Italian city in Mediterranean trade during the period covered in this chapter was:
    a. Florence
    b. Genoa
    c. Rome
    d. Venice

9. The devastation of the bubonic plague led to social unrest in Europe, because:
    a. The death of so many peasants resulted in a shortage of food
    b. The Mediterranean trade with Asia was interrupted
    c. Peasants and workers who survived agitated for higher wages and more mobility
    d. Peasants and workers who survived had lost faith in the ability of their rulers to protect them

10. Which of the following was <u>not</u> an important reason for Europe's urban economic revival in the later Middle Ages?
    a. Increased agricultural productivity
    b. The end of Viking raids
    c. The Crusades
    d. The formation of guilds

11. Amerigo Vespucci's most important contribution to the "Age of Discovery" was:
    a. His discovery of the South American coastline
    b. His discovery that the Americas were not part of Asia
    c. His discovery of the Pacific Ocean
    d. His discovery of a sea route to India

12. The Vikings were people from _____, who raided, traded, and settled along European coasts and rivers during the early Middle Ages.
    a. Scandinavia
    b. Normandy
    c. Russia
    d. Iceland

13. Jews were prominent in European economic activity until:
    a. Viking raids on cities and ports ceased
    b. The Christian Church eased its prohibitions on interest on loans
    c. Portuguese traders began making inroads in the Indian Ocean trade
    d. Renaissance humanist began persecuting them

14. The first European expedition to sail completely around the world was led by:
    a. James Cook
    b. Amerigo Vespucci
    c. Abel Tasman
    d. Ferdinand Magellan

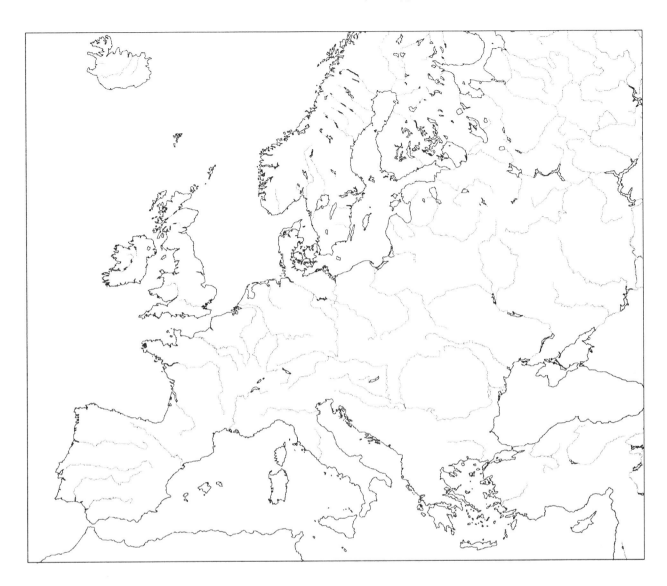

1. On the map above, locate the following:
   a. The original homeland of the Vikings and their principal areas of activity
   b. Areas under Muslim control during the early Middle Ages
   c. The flowing cities: Florence, Genoa, Venice, Lisbon, Constantinople, Rome

2. On the map above, locate or trace the following:
    a. The routes of Columbus, Magellan, Dias, da Gama, and Vespucci
    b. Areas that were under Spanish and Portuguese control by 1600
    c. The ports of Ceuta, Vera Cruz, Mombasa, Goa, Malacca, and Manila

STUDY QUESTIONS: Consider the following questions carefully. Be prepared to supply specific evidence and examples to support your points in a class discussion or a concise, well-organized written essay.

1. The chapter discusses no fewer than five important social, political and cultural consequences of the flowering of the European economy from the 11th through the 15th centuries C.E. List as many of these consequences as you can and then review at least two of them in detail, explaining specifically <u>how</u> economic growth brought about the political, social or cultural change under discussion.

2. Compare the flourishing economies of Mongol and Ming China (Chapter 12) with that of later medieval and Renaissance Europe. In what ways were they similar? In what ways did they differ? Are there any indications in the text that the European economy might overtake that of China in the period after 1500?

3. According to the text, Jews had become "so much a part of the merchant classes in early medieval northern Europe that a traditional administrative phrase referred to 'Jews and other merchants'." Why was this the case? What were the effects of this on the status of Jews in Christian Europe?

HOW DO WE KNOW?

The following questions are based on the various illustrations or quotations and extracts from primary source documents and historical interpretations in the chapter.

1. The European Renaissance and the philosophy of humanism are often described in secular (non-religious) terms, but a good argument could be made that Christian religious influences were just as important as worldly ones in the origins and development of the Renaissance. Discuss this argument in an essay in which you cite evidence and examples from the text and illustrations in the chapter.

2. Discuss the advantages and disadvantages of Fernand Braudel's approach to history (p. 431), as opposed to the traditional focus on specific nations or societies; or on political and diplomatic history. What sorts of things might Braudel and his disciples, such as K.N. Chaudhuri focus upon, that other historians might overlook.

3. Discuss the influence of Muslim and Jewish writers such as Ibn Sina (Avicenna) and Ibn Rushd (Averroes) on European thought. What factors facilitated this interaction? What factors may account for its termination?